cases in
organizational and
administrative behavior

cases in organizational and administrative behavior

ROBERT E. C. WEGNER

Associate Professor of Administration

University of Saskatchewan

LEONARD SAYLES

Professor of Business Administration

Columbia University

Graduate School of Business

PRENTICE-HALL, INC., Englewood Cliffs, New Jersey

13–118562–4

Library of Congress Catalog Card Number: 71–158913

Printed in the United States of America

Current Printing (last digit):

10   9   8   7   6   5   4

PRENTICE-HALL INTERNATIONAL, INC., *London*
PRENTICE-HALL OF AUSTRALIA, PTY. LTD., *Sydney*
PRENTICE-HALL OF CANADA, LTD., *Toronto*
PRENTICE-HALL OF INDIA PRIVATE LIMITED, *New Delhi*
PRENTICE-HALL OF JAPAN, INC., *Tokyo*

to
renate and risha

preface

The cases which follow have been designed for use with standard texts in organizational and administrative behavior. They should prove particularly helpful in courses such as organizational behavior, human relations, individual and group behavior, supervision, personnel administration, management, industrial psychology, and the sociology of organizations.

All of the cases are based on the reports of actual participants; none are contrived. They have been selected with the purpose of helping the reader to appreciate the wide range of human problems faced by different kinds of organizations in diverse settings. Some of the cases involve routine manual jobs; others, highly complex tasks. All types of employees are represented—from the semi-skilled blue collar worker to the top executive; from the clerk to the research specialist. Some of the cases are purposely short and involve a somewhat simple problem; others delve deeply into very complex issues. The multinational corporation provides the setting for some of the cases; the small family-owned business for others. Some of the cases deal with governmental agencies; several deal with organizations in foreign countries.

We have long felt that the typical manager deals with challenges and dilemmas in his daily activities that are far more complex and difficult than would seem obvious. By reflecting these challenges and dilemmas in our cases, we hope to impart a feeling for the real world of work with all its complexities, subtleties, and excitement. We also feel that the realness of these cases will serve to illustrate and amplify the more constrained concepts of textbooks in the area. The analysis of the questions at the end of the cases is designed to involve the reader in exactly the type of decision-making under conflict and uncertainty that confronts the manager in his job. In summary, these cases are designed as vicarious participations in a wide variety of management decisions involving human beings under stress.

We gratefully acknowledge the help of our students and colleagues whose ideas and suggestions formed the basis for many of the cases in this text. Our secretaries Darleen Bellamy and Fanny Williams helped us greatly; and a special note of thanks to Shirley Wenger and Renate Wegner who typed the final manuscript. We would also like to express our graditude to Jerry Miller of Stanford University and Gerald Bell of the University of North Carolina for their suggestions.

ROBERT E. C. WEGNER
Regina, Saskatchewan

LEONARD SAYLES
Hartsdale, New York

how to use this book

WHAT IS MEANT BY A CASE

In developing this book we often found ourselves questioning the very use of the word "case." We felt that "case" frequently denotes ponderous reams of somewhat dull material which very often appears contrived and manipulated to make a specific point. Such cases more often reflect the astute preciseness of the writer than actual situations in the real world. Although this type of case has relevance to certain types of material, we feel that cases in human behavior should be based on actual incidents and thus have made a strong effort to avoid the typical dilemma-oriented case. It would be just as meaningful to call our cases "vignettes," "incidents," or even "anecdotes." While some of the cases are quite long and do indeed involve dilemmas, the point is that these dilemmas are actual occurrences and have not been placed there to make a specific point.

HOW TO ANALYZE THE CASES

Since the cases reflect the real work situation with all its complexities and subtleties, it is impossible to suggest a strategy for analysis that will invariably succeed. An attempt to diagram the case, looking at the actors, the action, and the consequences of their interaction, might prove helpful in some cases. The use of a problem-solving schema (identifying the problem, examining the various alternatives, selecting the best alternative, implementing that alternative, evaluating the implementation, and so forth) will work for other cases. Because the cases involve a slice of organizational life, the problems are often disturbingly hidden and frustratingly difficult to analyze by any rigid system.

However, the cases must be analyzed. How, then, is it to be accomplished? We feel that the student will be most successful if he simply asks himself the following questions as he works through the case. First, what happened in the case? In attempting to answer this question, he should make a conscious effort to emphasize the behavioral description of events, that is, the who, what, where, and when of the situation. It is risky to try to answer the why of the situation first. There is a temptation to immediately impart motivation to the various actors' behaviors; this emphasis on the motivational aspects might cause the student to overlook the important cultural, structural, and technological aspects that may have a very crucial impact on what has happened. Once the student has carefully described, in behavioral terms, what has happened, he can then turn to the second question: why did it happen? Again the student should guard against making an *a priori* judgment of the cause of behavior and be sure to take into account all the variables that may affect behavior: personality, cultural background, education, environment, technology, group pressure, and so on. The final question in the analysis is: what can be done to alleviate the problem? The caution here is to be certain that whatever is suggested is operationally feasible. Can the solution be implemented? This question, often overlooked, is crucial to the solution of any organizational situation and should be an integral part of any student's decision-making ability when he enters the real world.

By elaborating on the analysis of these cases, we do not wish to prejudice other attempts and methods made by either the instructor or the student. At one point in the development of this book we had considered not giving any specific guidelines on how to analyze the cases for fear of jeopardizing the creativity of the individual instructor or student using these cases. We strongly suggest that continuous experimentation take place in the attempt to analyze the materials presented.

The questions at the end of each case are designed to provide a starting point for the analysis of what happened, why it happened, and what can be done. However, it must be emphasized that these questions are only meant to serve as the starting point for discussion of the cases. We do not mean to infer that these are the only questions which should be discussed or even that they are the most important questions. We hope that they are provocative enough to stimulate further questions and excursions into subsidiary areas of organizational behavior. Of course, it should be added, there are no right or wrong answers; the complexities of the issues raised in many of the cases defy simple answers. The student will no doubt be frustrated in his attempt to find the "right" answer. This frustration is meant to serve an instructional purpose in that it further typifies the type of situation the student will face as a manager. Unfortunately, there are very seldom clearly defined and easily evaluated "right" and "wrong" answers in the area of human behavior, particularly in organizational life.

If the complaint should arise that there is not sufficient information given to deal with the cases, we remind the student that the typical manager seldom has all the information he would like to have before the various pressures of his job force him into making a decision. A related dilemma is that when the information is the most scanty, the possibility for action is greatest; when the information is most complete, the possibility for action is most limited. The manager has to learn how to make this trade-off between degree of knowledge and possibility for action. The student, in having to make decisions under uncertainty (incomplete knowledge), will be getting very realistic training for the type of decisions he will have to make in the future, no matter what the organization. In sum, we feel that the lack of clear-cut answers and the incompleteness of information is conducive to learning what life will be like in the world of organizations.

HOW TO USE THE PHYSICAL FORMAT OF THE TEXT

The physical format of the text is designed to help the student analyze the cases and answer the questions at the end of the cases. To get the most out of a case, it has to be more than read: it must be read, re-read, dissected, torn apart, looked at again, left aside, read again, *ad infinitum*. In contrast to straight textual material, then, a case has to be more than "read through;" it must be "worked through." To facilitate this activity, the pages have been designed with extra-size margins so that the student can make notes, draw diagrams, pencil in questions, add points of criticism, voice disagreements, and, quite literally, "work through" the case. We feel that the experience will provide him with a meaningful and productive encounter with each case, and one that is again quite realistic—the manager confronted with a human problem does not see it written up as a case but must "work through" it as it happens. In copying the activity of the manager, the student is getting more training for the future.

We feel the student will have the best results with each case if he in general, uses the following method of analysis: (1) quickly read through the case; (2) carefully review the questions at the end of the case; (3) re-read the case thoroughly with the questions in mind; (4) begin to work through the case, making notes and comments in the margins as indicated above and, continuously referring to the questions, re-reading sections as necessary; and (5) writing out the answers to the questions at the end of the case, making notes about any additional questions or issues he would like to raise in class when the case is discussed.

To aid both the instructor and the student in using this text, we have included a matrix (see pg. xiii), indicating the title of each case on the vertical axis and the organizational setting along with the concepts dealt with in each case on the horizontal axis. The uses of this matrix are varied. For instance, the instructor may decide that he would like the sequence of cases to parallel his lecture-discussion sessions on major concepts in the management of organizations. This might entail using the "group behavior" cases first, particularly cases 7 and 9 (in which this is a major issue), and also considering some of the eight other cases noted in the matrix in which this is a subsidiary issue. Next, the class might deal with "status relationships," which is the primary focus in cases 5 and 11. A special problem in both the group and status areas is "professionalization," on which case 4 concentrates.

Depending on textbook selection and instructor preferences, such sequences are subject to wide variation; therefore, the ordering of cases in the volume does *not* reflect any ideal sequence. The instructor, for example, may decide that he would like to deal with those cases which involve foreign operations; therefore, cases 5, 26, and 28 would be assigned. Or perhaps the instructor would like to deal with small business organizations and thus would assign cases 13, 15, and 20. He could also combine organizational settings with given concepts. For instance, if the instructor decides that he would like to look at conflict in military organizations, he would assign cases 8, 11, and 23. Or he might want to examine group behavior in manufacturing organizations, so cases 7, 10, and 31 would be assigned. Obviously, the combinations are almost limitless and the degree of latitude for the individual instructor is vast. The individual student may use the matrix to work ahead in the text or to examine cases relevant to a term paper or essay that he is writing.

How the instructor wants to utilize the cases in conjunction with his course is for him to decide. One of the ways we have used the cases is in a three session-a-week format where the first two days are used for lecturing and discussing materials assigned in the text or reader, and the case is assigned for the third class session to help illustrate what has been developed in the lectures. Conversely, the instructor may wish to lecture for several sessions and then take a number of sessions to discuss a whole group of cases. Again, the choice is only limited by the ingenuity of the instructor and his students. To facilitate discussion, we have sometimes broken the class into groups of students with each group then being assigned a particular question from the case. To see what different types of issues are raised, the same question might be assigned to several individuals or groups. But no matter what method is used, we feel that the student, by using these cases, will develop a more sophisticated and realistic view of the types of situations that the typical manager faces in his day-to-day activities.

	authority	change	communication	conflict	controls, rules, quotas	coordination	delegation	discipline	foreign operations	group behavior	hierarchical relations	job satisfaction	lateral relations	leadership	personality	personnel training and development	professionalization	racial conflict	specialization	status relationships	supervision	unions
1												X	✓		✓	✓					✓	
2												X										
3				X															✓		✓	
4		✓															X		✓		✓	
5			✓							✓	✓					✓	✓		X			
6		X				✓											✓				✓	
7										X		✓						✓			✓	
8			X			✓				✓									✓			
9		✓	✓							X									✓		✓	✓
10		✓	X	✓						✓									✓			
11	✓		✓							✓									X		✓	
12							✓										✓					X
13			✓			✓	X			✓											✓	
14						✓															X	
15						✓								✓	✓						X	
16																	✓		✓		X	
17	✓	✓				✓	✓					✓	✓	X		✓						
18														X								
19	X				✓					✓		✓		✓								
20	X					✓						✓			✓							
21					✓			X													✓	
22											X		✓		✓						✓	
23		✓	✓							✓									X			
24		✓			X					✓		✓	✓			✓	✓			✓	✓	
25				✓	X	✓															✓	
26							✓					X	✓							✓		
27			✓	✓	✓	✓				✓		X					✓			✓		
28	✓		✓			✓		X				✓	✓								✓	
29						✓						X							✓			
30	✓											✓			X						✓	
31					✓		✓			✓	X					✓						
32		✓				X	✓					✓	✓									

X = major issue;   ✓ = subsidiary issues

	Case	**Organizational Setting**
1	elaine, the harassed secretary	*insurance company*
2	three "clericals"	*bank*
3	making quota	*insurance company*
4	operations research stubs its toe in retailing	*retail*
5	the eager new lawyer and the managing clerk	*law firm*
6	a change in the editorial department	*publisher*
7	bad times come to hanesville	*manufacturer*
8	conflict at sea	*military*
9	the luggers versus the butchers	*food processer*
10	the machinists	*manufacturer*
11	the repair ship	*military*
12	two troublesome union-management cases	*manufacturer/publishers*
13	the troubles at wilson	*small business*
14	two head nurses: a study in contrast	*hospital*
15	ron, the steel man	*small business*
16	terry, the disappearing supervisor	*consulting firm*
17	chuck, the manager	*manufacturer*
18	summer camp	*military*
19	evolution in the mailroom	*food processer*
20	the job change	*small business*
21	barney and the coding department	*food processer*
22	diary of a failure	*opinion research firm*
23	the old "new" pilots	*military*
24	the fate of the underwriters	*insurance company*
25	trouble at the loading docks	*manufacturer*
26	growth at shamrock	*insurance company*
27	conflict at a research and development laboratory	*government research*
28	management problems in india	*manufacturer*
29	introducing a new appliance model	*manufacturer*
30	cynthia, the supervisor	*bank*
31	the jungle at foam brewing	*manufacturer*
32	a new division	*metals processer*

table of contents

cases in
organizational and
administrative behavior

elaine,
the harassed secretary

PART ONE: THE INCIDENT

Sometime, just before noon on a rainy day in April 1966, an attractive twenty-three-year-old secretary named Elaine got up from her desk in a small insurance agency in New England, went up to the office manager's desk and said, "May I go home? I am sick—sick of all this." With a wide sweep of her hand she indicated the office and the girls working in it. Without waiting for a reply she spun around and stomped out of the building, jumped into her new light-blue Mercury, and recklessly drove out of the parking lot.

PART TWO: A GIRL AND HER WORK

Having graduated from high school in 1961, and having completed secretarial school during the summer, Elaine was ready to go to work for the National Mutual Life Insurance Company in their home office by late fall. During the period since her graduation, Elaine had discovered a great deal of extra time on her hands. Although basically an energetic girl, she "wasted" (as she put it) a lot of time in school sitting around talking and visiting with her girl friends. By the time secretarial school was over and she had gone to work for National Mutual (hereafter NML) she had lost contact with many of her friends. However, she retained a small group of close friends whom she saw frequently during her free time.

Elaine came from a lower middle-income family and

was one of two children. Her older married sister was experiencing personal problems and appeared to be headed for the divorce court. Elaine seldom saw her father for he was constantly on the road. Although she spent a good deal of time with her mother, she was seldom home long enough to talk with her for any great length of time. But her mother followed Elaine's life very closely—incessantly advising, always reading her mail—and was completely involved in a sympathetic but outspoken way in Elaine's social and work life. Elaine, who usually complained when her independence was infringed upon, seemed to accept her mother's behavior as normal and quite permissible.

Although there were many girls of Elaine's age at the home office of NML, she rarely joined them in off-work activities. During this period she joined a women's bowling league, but not the one that consisted of NML employees.

In the winter of 1963 she began negotiations with another NML office for employment, and in May 1964 she started work at a new regional office that was in the same town as the home office but located closer to her home. Now, instead of working with a group of 30 to 40 women, she found herself working with only nine other women mostly older than she. Instead of lunching in a huge cafeteria, at a table with ten or more girls of her own age, she now usually ate alone.

At the home office her work consisted of typing letters in response to certain types of queries by policyholders. These letters were always dictated by the same man. In her new job she typed life insurance estate programs as well as various letters dictated by four different men. Two of these men arrived at the office by 8:30 in the morning, and were ready to dictate to Elaine when she arrived at 9:00. Usually she was finished with dictation by 10:30. She took a fifteen-minute coffee break, then came back to run the switchboard. When the men returned at 1:00 P.M. from field work, she would leave for lunch which she usually had at home.

No formal rules existed regulating hours of employment in the agency, so the days were often either longer or shorter than a typical office job and depended on the work load. Elaine's routine was seldom the same each day. Often there were periods when she would sit and chat with the agents as they related the activities of their

2

day and listened to her stories of things she had done or heard regarding her social life or the company and agency. All in all, Elaine was quite pleased with her new job.

In 1964, Elaine became secretary of her bowling league, and the recording of scores and typing of schedules required about seven hours each week. Four evenings a week she worked as a waitress in a nearby ice cream shop. Between the job at the insurance agency and the work at the ice cream shop, Elaine was earning nearly $125.00 a week. Since she lived at home, her daily expenses were minimal. Thus, with each passing month, her bank account grew larger as she continued to work at two jobs. She lived at home, went out on dates, and ran her bowling league. Elaine, it appeared, not only had a good life, but also possessed the abundant energy and vitality with which to enjoy it.

PART THREE: A GIRL AND HER FRIENDS

Although not a very religious girl Elaine usually went to church each Sunday, accompanied by two or three of her girlfriends. These, however, were not the same girls with whom she bowled. She rarely saw her bowling friends when she was at parties or on double dates. Her "party" friends were neither school friends nor work associates, although she did spend some of her "fun" time with a few of the young people with whom she worked at the ice cream shop.

Of the nine women in the office, only two others were single. The rest were middle-aged, but they were, in spirit, young and "swingers." Nevertheless, Elaine's relationship with them was one of cordiality and respect but not close. She was not overfond of them as a group, but she indicated that she did not individually dislike any of them. She neither saw nor kept in touch with any of her old associates at the home office, and had made few friends in the two years that she was there. Despite the impression this might convey, Elaine was really a gregarious and friendly girl. She had a large number of friends drawn from each of her "crowds." Elaine seemed to be leading many different lives at the same time.

When she arrived at the office in the morning, it was not unusual for Elaine to find waiting at her desk one of the four agents for whom she worked. The reason, of course, was that the agents made money out in the field,

3

and not in dictating or sitting behind their desks involved in paper work. Thus their objective was to get their desk work out of the way as soon as possible and then go out in the field. To make a sale, the agent first had to find a name, usually from the existing list; then a standard form introduction letter was sent out. These were sent at the rate of about 25 or 30 a week. He could also have a direct mailing list typed and sent to the home office where form letters were mailed out, then contact these people by phone and attempt to make appointments with them. After an appointment, the agent would send the customer a short note of appreciation with the assurance that he had begun work on his program. After another round of telephone calls and appointments, the sale was made. On the average, if an agent sold two policies a week he would have sent out 90 pieces of mail.

Elaine's work load varied from about 100 to 140 pieces a week. The agents felt that the more they could individually get from Elaine in the way of work, the higher their sales volume would be. Thus they competed for her time; and since there were no set rules governing the amount of work that could be requested, they would usually give her more than she could possibly do and hope that a larger portion would be completed than they had expected. Often they were amazed when all their work was completed. When this happened, however, it was not unusual for them to fail to follow up on it and Elaine's work would be wasted. Elaine was understandably chagrined by this.

The agents, besides competing for Elaine's time, also competed among themselves, and in many instances Elaine found herself in the middle of a feud. There were also certain months in the year when business picked up markedly. Usually these occurred at the beginning of a year, during the July and November campaigns, just prior to agents' vacations, and before holidays. During these periods, the agents put even greater pressure on Elaine to get the work done. In addition there were occasions when the agents lost large cases or became depressed over extended slump periods, and as a result made extremely unreasonable requests for work from their secretaries. Many times this rush work would be completed and then collect dust on the salesmen's desks for hours, and sometimes days. This further aggravated Elaine who, because of her skill, did most of the rush work.

4

One day, Elaine was interrupted while typing a letter, and asked to do a rush program for one of the usually "rushing" agents. Fifteen minutes later she completed the program and laid it on his desk. During this particular month, with income taxes due, the work tended to slow down a great deal. In addition, the secretaries noticed an increase in requests for favors that usually involved some "special" work or "fast" delivery—which actually were neither so special nor needed so quickly by the agents. When she saw the rush program the next morning, still with the carbons attached lying on the agent's desk, Elaine realized that this was one of those "favors."

She was also involved during this time with a great number of standard preapproach letters but had continually been forced to put them off because of interruptions to do favors. The prospective customers' names would be given to her on Monday, and the letters had to be typed by Thursday evening. She usually spaced the typing evenly each day, but in this case she had to do them all on Thursday.

While she was working at the ice cream shop on Wednesday, her manager called her in and indicated that some of the other waitresses had complained because she was pushing her orders through, that is, placing her orders at the front of the line. He also said that she probably did this because she felt rushed by impatient customers, but that the real problem was that she spent too much time talking and chatting with her friends who often came into the shop. He warned Elaine not to socialize so much. Elaine liked the manager, but felt that he was a little unfair in this criticism in that the other waitresses always talked with their friends too. After work that night, Elaine attended a large party where she soothed her feelings by drinking a bit too much.

The following day, Thursday, the office manager at the agency noticed her talking on the phone while she was typing the standard form letters. Elaine often did this because it seemed to make typing these letters more bearable. The office manager pointed out that some of the agents had complained about her work, and that the probable reason for this was her talking on the phone while working.

Elaine's mood that morning was not amenable to such

5

criticism. In the first place, she had a slight hangover from the night before and this caused her to make mistakes she would not have normally made. Second, she was still somewhat hurt by the criticism of the manager of the ice cream shop—whom she admired a great deal. Third, the weather was rainy and as miserable as she herself felt. None of the agents had shown up for work because of the bad weather and the normal slow operations at this time of the year. This upset Elaine because she wanted to tell them about the party she had attended. In addition the rest of the office staff was also in a bad mood, and her complaining manager, who was a large forty-eight-year-old woman, was just typical of the atmosphere of the day.

By eleven o'clock she felt that she could type the standard letters in her sleep, even though she could not type them correctly. Finally she made one mistake too many, ripped the letter from her typewriter, grabbed her coat, and told the office manager she was leaving. This was a complete surprise to the office manager. She had many times seen girls go into the powder room to get their problems ironed out by an unscheduled rest, but had never seen a girl simply get up and leave. Elaine's actions left her speechless and without a clue as to what her own action should be.

Discussion Questions

1. Analyze the factors which led to Elaine's action. Do you think her reaction was typical? Why? Discuss other reactions to pressures on the job.

2. If you were Elaine's immediate supervisor, what would you have done when she made her announcement? Do you think that something could have been done at this point? Why?

3. What do you think is going to happen to Elaine next? Do you think she will come back, or will she quit? Why?

4. Assume that Elaine does quit, and you decide that she is too good to lose and you want to get her back. How would you go about trying to convince her to return? What type of counseling would you give her? (Assume you are the office manager.)

5. Suppose Elaine doesn't return and that a week

later you, as her supervisor, receive a phone call asking for a recommendation for her in a similar type job. What would your recommendation be?

6. *Do you think that Elaine's relationship with her co-workers was a good one? Discuss. Would Elaine be easy or difficult to work with? Why?*

7. *Are there any background factors in Elaine's personal life that would have led you to possibly expect such behavior? If so, what are they?*

8. *Analyze the work-flow relationship in the office in which Elaine worked. If you were to make any changes in the organization of the office, what would they be?*

9. *Do you think NML is being run effectively? If not, what suggestions would you make for improvement?*

2

three "clericals"

In the period of time I worked in the Foreign Department of the Wall Street Bank, I got a chance to closely observe the operations of three "clericals"—Joe Apprendi, Lou Costello, and Bill Sarazin. The following analysis of the work of these young men aptly illustrates how misleading the term clerical was in describing their on-the-job behavior.

JOE: THE DOCUMENT CHECKER

In negotiating a letter of credit, which is a form of loan extended in import-export financing, documents are required to certify shipment and receipt of the merchandise to be financed by a lending bank. The job of the document checker is to verify and process the various documents connected with the transactions. The formal description of the duties involved is as follows:

The document checker receives the documents sent to the bank and logs them in a record ledger, indicating the time and date received. The documents are then broken down, and their number and contents are checked against the requirements stipulated in the original letter of credit agreement. The checker must make certain that the commercial invoice correctly describes the merchandise to be shipped, and that the bills of lading show clear title to the goods. If these documents are found to be faulty in any respect, the bank will not honor the negotiation and return the documents to the presenting party. If the articles are in compliance with the original requirements they are processed by the document checker, with charges and lending rates calculated and applied. Once this has been accomplished the documents, along with an attached work sheet, are presented to a departmental officer for his approval and signature.

Joe Apprendi serves as the principal document checker in the Letter of Credit Section. Joe is twenty-nine years old, married, and has one son. He attended college for two semesters, but for financial reasons was not able to continue. Joe is intelligent, has a warm personality, and has developed close personal relationships with members of the department. Since he joined the bank, his advancement in the Foreign Department has been rapid. He has held the present position of document checker for approximately three years.

Joe Apprendi has made his job quite different from its official description. His ability to converse with all types of individuals has made him the acknowledged spokesman for the workers in the department. He interacts with a large number of individuals not connected with the normal work-flow relationships of a document checker. In fact, he answers general questions about the department's procedures to customers who telephone and those who came to the bank personally. Joe also supplies information to other bank personnel concerned with legal procedures in foreign business dealings.

Joe, on his own initiative, has taken numerous courses in marine cargo and insurance laws. He has become so skilled in handling technical documents that it is recognized that he knows this area better than any other member of the department. He consults with officers and staff of other departments as to their functions and operational procedures. By taking an interest in outside areas, Joe has acquired many new and useful associations.

In other words, Joe has made himself invaluable to the Foreign Department. When loaning officers return from overseas trips they initially talk to Joe about how the department has been functioning in their absence even though there are operational officers available. These same loaning officers are so confident of Joe's abilities that they have included him in high-level conferences concerned with future departmental business. And whenever there is a procedural question as to the format of a letter of credit for a customer, the answer always seems to be, "Ask Joe, he'll know for sure." The fact is that Joe usually does know, and recently he has been granted the authority to make the final approval on documents without an additional signature.

It is interesting to note that Joe's immediate superior has considerably reduced his contact with the workers of the department, and this officer concentrates, almost exclusively, on new nonoperational projects. This has reached the point where Joe, with the officer's approval and gratitude, now handles the majority of personnel problems among the secretarial and clerical staffs of the department.

LOU: THE PAYING AND RECEIVING TELLER

In almost every large economical bank, and certainly in all foreign departments, there is a section concerned mainly with paying out and receiving various items in foreign currencies. The name of this position in the Foreign Department of the Wall Street Bank is the Foreign Paying and Receiving Teller, and the specific description of this job is as follows:

In negotiating items of foreign currencies, the teller's method of payment and form of receipt include checks and mail and cable transfers. When an item is sufficiently large, provision must be made with the officers of the department for an additional buying in the currency markets. The majority of payments and receipts are in the form of mail items, and many payments need only be "charged to" or "credited to" accounts held with the bank. If the items are payable abroad only by foreign currency, then the item is sent out on a collection basis and proceeds are credited only when the collection is confirmed. If payment is to be made through a foreign bank, the transfer will be placed through a correspondent bank. The correspondent is determined by a departmental officer from a preferential list.

Lou Costello is the Paying and Receiving Teller. Like Joe Apprendi, he is the son of Italian-born parents. He is forty years old, married, and has no children. Before joining the Wall Street Bank, he worked in several other foreign departments of large New York banks. His education extends only through the high-school level, but Lou is quick and efficient in his work and has acquired valuable instincts for dealing with rapid fluctuations in foreign exchange trading. He is a close personal friend of Joe's, and they have recently moved into the same neighborhood in Brooklyn. Lou's outgoing personality is somewhat overbearing at times, but generally he is well liked and his nine years of experience in the department is highly regarded by his fellow workers.

Lou Costello has become something more than a Paying and Receiving Teller. Lou's skill has made him the exchange dealer, not just for the Foreign Department but for the entire bank. Originally, all exchange transactions had to be approved by an officer before a buy or sell was made. Now Lou has been given the authority not only for initiating the transaction, but for maintaining what he feels are the correct current balances for the amounts of currency required by the bank. Because of his outgoing nature he has come to personally know many individuals in various trading institutions, and his list of contacts is of vital importance to the department.

Lou's friendship with Joe has given Lou a detailed knowledge of the Letter of Credit Section, and he has reciprocated by teaching Joe the fundamentals of exchange trading. The department head has come to rely on their ability to "cover" for one another. In fact the two men have become an efficient and independent unit that can handle almost all phases of the department's operational work, and have done so during vacation periods. Initially the Paying and Receiving Teller was only one of several in a separate department, but now Lou is the department. His advice is constantly being sought by management, and, like Joe, he has been permitted to sign numerous credentials and documents with the authority of an officer. Furthermore, it is his decision alone as to which correspondent will get the commissions on a particular negotiation.

BILL: THE BOOKKEEPER

In each department of a bank certain records must be maintained. This is the essential function of the bookkeeper in the Foreign Department. His duties are defined as follows:

The primary responsibility of the bookkeeper is to post the liability ledgers which cover the transactions of the entire department. Posting is the operation of recording credits and debits to the proper accounts, and then applying the transaction tickets to general bookkeeping records. On a daily basis, the tickets are submitted to a central proof section with a summary report. Also the bookkeeper must check the subsidiary ledgers against control ledgers. Individual accounts related to various sections of the department are checked weekly against the subsidiary and control ledgers. Finally, the bookkeeper must maintain a record of outstanding foreign loans for each week.

Bill Sarazin serves as the bookkeeper for the Foreign Department. He is of Slavic descent, twenty-one years old, recently married, and now lives in New Jersey. Bill finished high school, and for several years has been taking college-level courses at night. He has been employed by the bank for only a little more than a year, but has quickly mastered the bookkeeping and posting machines.

Bill's quiet nature and diligent attitude have made him a popular worker, and he has achieved rapid acceptance with all members of the department. In particular, Bill has become closely associated with Joe Apprendi and Lou Costello. They often meet socially after hours.

Bookkeeping, more than the other jobs described, seems to be a truly routine occupation, yet Bill Sarazin is definitely not a routine bookkeeper. The mechanics of the job are relatively simple. But when problem accounts create difficulties, the job quickly expands; and when it does, it must be held by an individual with initiative and insight. Bill is such a person, and because of his excellent performance under stress he serves as an effective bridge between management and the accounting records. His ability at "troubleshooting" is really a result of self-education. Like Joe and Lou, he has become interested in the operations of other sections. By learning the procedures within sections he can now quickly spot errors and anticipate problem areas. In this respect, his contributions have resulted in major revisions in the bookkeeping methods employed by the department.

Since Bill has become friends with Joe and Lou he now spends much of his spare time in their sections. Joe has responded by instructing him in processing documents, and when the flow of work is particularly heavy the management has requested Bill to act as a document checker. He has been able to take on this additional task because his speed at posting has drastically cut the time normally required for the operation. Bill has become so proficient at this "emergency job" of checking documents that Joe rarely has to do more with his work than add a signature.

Above all, Bill has altered his position because he performs so effectively in critical situations. When problems arose with previous bookkeepers there was inevitably a cluster of officers around the posting machines. But the quality of his work is such that the officers' concern with bookkeeping matters has been greatly reduced. This has won him the respect of those officers, and as a result of his reputation they now come to him with an increasing number of special and urgent projects which are unrelated to his normal duties.

The three individuals described above differ in many respects, but they share certain basic feelings about the bank. They all were extremely loyal to the Foreign Department, and, as a result, wanted to remain with the Wall Street Bank.

It is interesting to note that within a fairly short period of time, Joe Apprendi left the bank to become a state bank examiner; Lou Costello left the bank to join the Foreign Exchange Division of another large New York City bank; and Bill Sarazin quit working altogether in order to continue his college education on a full-time basis.

Discussion Questions

1. Work satisfies different needs in different people. Analyze the type of needs you think were relevant to the behavior of Joe Apprendi, Lou Costello, and Bill Sarazin.

2. Do you think that the behavior of these three "clericals" is typical or atypical for men in their position? Why?

3. What factors in the bank environment affected the work behavior of Joe, Lou, and Bill? How?

4. Rewrite the formal job descriptions given to adequately reflect what Joe, Lou, and Bill really did.

5. Suppose someone examined your response to question four and said, "The only problem with the original job descriptions was that the Wall Street Bank did not keep them up to date." What would your reaction be to this comment?

6. Of what use are job descriptions? How do they enhance or inhibit performance on the job?

7. To what extent do you think the different personalities of Joe, Lou and Bill affected their performance on the job?

8. Describe the interactions between Joe, Lou, and Bill. In what way are they beneficial to the Wall Street Bank? Is there any way in which they can be considered detrimental? How?

9. Can you speculate as to the reason Joe, Lou, and Bill left the Wall Street Bank? Were the reasons totally external to the bank, or do you think that something about the operations of the bank induced them to leave? Explain your reasoning.

10. How do you think the Foreign Department of the Wall Street Bank will function now that the three "clericals" have left? Why? Do you think their leaving is a positive or negative action with regards to the operations of the Foreign Department? Why?

3

making quota

The National Life Insurance Company regularly employs approximately 100 part-time personnel who work from 4:30 to 8:30 P.M. Monday through Friday. The workers are all men, and in order to qualify for the jobs they must be full-time university students. The work of these part-time personnel ranges in difficulty from such simple tasks as filing loan papers and taping extension stickers on policyholder account cards, to the complex operation of billing machines which require about four weeks' training. These workers are paid $2.16 per hour—a wage approximately 50% higher than those paid by other organizations for comparable part-time work. This wage was one of the attractions to these night-shift workers (as all those who work between 4:30 P.M. and 8:30 P.M. were called) in that they were trying to earn extra money for expenses.

The men who worked at night did exactly the same work as girls who worked the day shift, but the girls were paid a starting salary of only $60.00 per week, or the equivalent of $1.50 per hour. As a result of this, there was some conflict between the groups. The men often complained that the girls didn't get much done, and the girls resented the fact that they were paid so much less. However, the girls were given a half-hour coffee break every morning, free lunches, air conditioning, music, and the privilege to use the vending machines or go to the washroom whenever they desired. They also stopped work about 4:00 P.M. and socialized for the last half hour. Such socializing was masqueraded as an attempt to clean up and put things away, but the nonproductivity of this time was apparent to all. Management made no attempt to curb such practices.

In contrast, there was no music at night, the air conditioning was turned off, workers were not allowed to use the vending machines—although they could purchase candy or cigarettes before work, and eat or smoke on the job—and there were no breaks. Also the group worked steadily until 8:25 P.M. Management felt that college students were primarily interested in money, since the job was not a permanent position. Thus the company paid a high wage and cut expenses in other areas. Results seemed to validate this policy: productivity per man-hour was 30% higher than that for the day shift, and employee turnover was very low compared with that for most part-time jobs.

It is interesting to note, however, that during mid-semester and final exams absenteeism ran high among these night-shift workers, and productivity among those who did work was low. Using my own experience as a reference, during finals my output did not fall but my percentage of errors rose as high as 8%. Similar results were observable elsewhere.

For the ten months I worked with the company, I operated a billing machine which recorded the various figures that were to be included in the bill sent to each policyholder. The company practiced very close supervision on night-shift workers. Results for every job were judged on a quantative basis, and all jobs were assigned a minimum acceptable percentage of errors. My job as a machine operator was judged on this negative reward basis: I had to complete 720 units in four hours with no more than 1% errors. This quota was often very difficult to meet, especially on the nights when packs of cards were of more than average difficulty. The job was extremely boring, but still required close attention. It did not demand any deep thought, and was not challenging or stimulating. Many workers who could not take the monotony of the job were shifted to other departments.

In order to counter the drudgery of the job, I developed what might be called a "game." Each pack usually contained 180 policyholders' account cards. About 150 of these had to be billed on two types of short forms—a #1 form and a #2 form. The number of each type billed was recorded on a digital index on the machine. Usually each pack had about the same number of each of the two types, and I played games of "basketball" with each pack with the #1's and the #2's. Usually the scores were quite close, and on a couple of occasions the game went into overtime—i.e., was continued with the next pack. Punching in the seven numbers that made up the policyholder's account number was equated with "dribbling the ball down the floor," and pushing in the button that rang up the total was equated with "putting the ball through the basket."

I became so accustomed to the high demands of the quota and the "basketball" game that when I was temporarily placed in another department where the quota was easier to attain I found that time passed very slowly and I was glad to return to the machine.

During the first month or so of work, there were 12 part-time employees who operated billing machines. As previously mentioned, the cards were split into packs of approximately 180 each. Cards of policyholders who had bought their policy within the past year did not have to be billed on the short forms because these forms recorded accumulated dividends, interest, and additional insurance obtained by "ploughing back" dividends to add to the size of the policy. Since it took one year for these benefits to accrue, new accounts did not have to be billed for these items; as a result, they represented "free" cards that counted toward one's quota.

On a night when there was a large number of "free" cards in a worker's packs he went above quota and, conversely, when there were no free cards he may have fallen below quota. As a result, operators who had the easier packs gave credit for some of their work to those who had difficult packs so that everyone finished the night above the quota. When a new worker joined the group, he was immediately informed of this policy.

By way of the daytime supervisors, management soon became aware of this practice through information provided by a first-line supervisor who had recently been promoted from his job as a machine operator. Management then instituted actions to try to prevent such practices.

First, the new supervisor was given orders to report anyone who engaged in "lending" or "borrowing" as a means of assuring that everyone made quota. Second, quota was raised from 720 (an already stringent quota) to 750 cards per night. The sudden clamp down by management coincided with the failure of three employees to return from vacation, and, rightly or wrongly, this was viewed as a form of revenge on the part of management. In addition, about this time, to facilitate work in another department, the pack size was cut from 180 and now varied between 90 and 160 cards per pack. This made quota even more difficult to reach, for about five minutes were required to total and rewrap each pack when it was completed, and the smaller pack size meant that more packs had to be completed per evening.

Thus quota was more difficult to reach, but management had left a loophole when it had packs wrapped within a range of 70 cards (i.e., between 90 and 160 cards per pack). This loophole was quickly seized by the employees. The number of cards in a pack was written in pencil on a slip of paper tucked into the packs; hence the employees recorded the pack number and the number of cards in the pack on their daily work slips, and the slips could easily be crosschecked by referring to the completed packs. However, workers began erasing the number of cards recorded by the daytime clerks and raising it by 15 or 20 and thus making it easier for them to reach quota.

This practice was carefully concealed from members of other groups, for if word of it ever got back to management it would have been easy for them to check and see that the total number of billings recorded for each agency often exceeded the number of policyholders in that agency. It was extremely unlikely that management would have checked this unless it were called to their attention. When I left the company, this "cheating" was still going on.

In some cases the company's strict concern with rules and procedures and seeming unconcern with employees' attitudes led to unfortunate occurrences. If an employee failed to meet his quota more than two or three times, he was usually dismissed. Since the part-time workers were not covered by any union agreement, there was little that could be done about such management action. On two other occasions a worker was fired during a week in which there was a holiday, thus the company did not have to pay him for the holiday. Whether this timing of the dismissals was intentional or not, it aroused suspicion among the other employees.

Also, during the early summer of the year I worked at National three employees were scheduled to take vacations. The workers had planned, for personal reasons, to quit after their vacation. A week before vacation one of them told me in confidence: "We're just going to take our vacation pay and never show up again. If we do tell them, they might fire us so they won't have to give us the paid vacation." As a result of this feeling and the workers' subsequent action the company lost three good men without notice, and work in their departments suffered. As I have noted above, this had other severe repercussions in that the management's subsequent raising of quota was viewed by the workers as retaliation for the failure of these three men to return after their vacation.

Discussion Questions

1. In what ways do the jobs of part-time workers differ from full-time workers? To the extent that antagonisms arise between these two groups, what can management do to alleviate them?

2. How does the status of night-shift workers differ from that of day-shift workers? What effect do you think this might have on the behavior of the workers?

3. What assumptions did the management of the National Life Insurance Company make concerning the motivations of the night and day shifts? Were these assumptions valid? Why? Would it be safe to assume that some workers are interested only in the economic rewards of their job? If so, what type of workers would they be?

4. In its structuring of the working conditions for the two shifts, could management be accused of manipulating the workers? If so, is this manipulation, by definition bad? Discuss.

5. How did the case writer overcome the boredom of the job? Is this a typical reaction? In what way could the case writer's "game" be dangerous? Discuss other ways workers attempt to overcome the boredom and monotony of their jobs. Have you ever done any of these? Are such attempts productive or counterproductive? Are there any circumstances under which boredom can be considered a positive aspect of a job?

6. Discuss the circular nature of the attempts by management and workers to either enforce or "make" quota. How successful was management's action? How could management have achieved productivity without resorting to quotas?

7. "National Life Insurance Company is a going concern. Their workers are highly paid, productive, and turnover is not unusually high. Their future success would appear assured." Do you agree with this statement? Discuss.

4

operations research
stubs its toe in retailing

Before going into the details of the case, a brief description of the Squires Company and the department concerned is necessary. The department is the Operations Research Department of Squires, a large retail store chain. Top management and other personnel in the organizational structure naturally emphasize the selling activity of the business. All other activities have become subservient to the goal of increasing the sales. As a result of this, recognition and reward have traditionally been linked to success in this area; consequently, store managers have been the prime source of future top executives of the corporation.

Recently, however, there has been some realization that increased profits are not only a result of increased sales, but also of improved operational efficiency. That is, a reduction in the operating costs in areas such as distribution and inventory control can increase the profit margin. Therefore an operations research department was added to the central staff.

This department has received several assignments involving inventory control and stock control, but is still not accepted by the oldtimers in company management who see it as a group of "whiz kids" who don't really understand retailing.

Most recently, the OR group was asked to develop some techniques to reduce bad debts, hopefully by improving the Credit Department's ability to evaluate customers' credit ratings and to decide when not to extend credit. The manager of the OR department, Gene, is very pleased about this assignment because it represents an extension of OR interest into an area that has heretofore been "out of bounds" for them.

He decided to give the primary responsibility to his best man, Don, a senior analyst. Don had been expecting to work full time in an area that was his special interest: capital budgeting and new corporate investments to facilitate financial planning in the company. Not only did Squires lack this important planning tool, but this was an area which could show very important and impressive results. Furthermore, it was a "hot" area in the professional OR and finance field. Some preliminary meetings with the finance people had convinced Gene that they were interested too.

Don accepted, although grudgingly, the assignment given him and began looking over the Credit Department. He found that the key person from whom he would have to obtain the basic data from which an OR "model" could be constructed was an employee of long service, Henry Cristo. Cristo had a fine reputation and seemed to work all the time. He even ate lunch at his desk, and stayed overtime almost every evening without compensation. Whereas the rest of the management group had college degrees, Cristo had not gone beyond high school. He had, however, mastered the intricacies of credit work and no one had any complaints about him.

The only problem Don had with Cristo was extracting information. Cristo treated everything as if it were top secret, and insisted that Don get written authorization for every data request he made. Don also discovered that many of the critical decision points in the department had never been written down and existed only in Cristo's head. When asked about these, Cristo always said it was very complicated and dependent on a lot of ill-defined factors. But he indicated his willingness to begin developing a "manual" containing the needed information. The manual "might" be done in a few months, if the work load of the department declined.

The more he worked on extracting bits and pieces of data, the more Don became convinced that this project wasn't fertile ground. More importantly, with all Cristo's defensiveness and idiosyncracies, it was a well-run department. Cristo not only worked hard, but he worked well. The chances of coming up with a formula that might save significant sums were small indeed, and the chances of having wasted several months of effort with nothing to show for it were great. This was frustrating to Don, who was ambitious and wanted to do things that were not only professionally exciting but would also show top management that he was a "comer." In a sales-dominated company like Squires it wasn't easy to get into management through a staff department, but Don was going to give it his best.

So Don reported to Gene that the project should be scrapped. Gene was enraged, ordered Don to stay with the project, and indicated that he had better "produce."

In order to understand Gene's heated reaction it is important to realize some of the pressures under which he has to work. He not only has to represent his group to the outside and elicit rewards for his group, but also has to "sell" operations research services to others. It is his job to contact and encourage people to use these services. Many times he has lectured on what OR can do for managers. In many ways Gene has had to educate managers to the tools of analysis available to them, and then convince the managers to use these tools. It is no small task to get a manager to budget money to study an area. This sometimes involves hours of persuasion.

Although Gene had to convince others to use OR, he knew that all problems are not interesting. Some are just plain dull and routine. Some are just pipe dreams. Many times, just to get "a foot in the door," Gene was forced to take on a poor project in the hope of being able to get a better one later. In addition there was considerable pressure from top management to work on rather "visible" issues, such as a bad-debt situation.

In Don's case, he would have rather been exploring "new" analysis in his specialty than applying past knowledge to cope with the immediate pragmatic problem which he viewed as unsolvable at the present time. In his view of the situation, he was being forced to choose between the futile pragmatic and the fruitful professional. When he was ordered to stick with the bad-debt project he saw all his avenues of advancement blocked.

Ironically, the value of an individual like Don to an organization is not only his ability to "produce" problem solutions; he must also come up with creative ideas. New ideas and theory lead to new applications. Always assigning and encouraging work on production problems may have a detrimental effect on the quality of analysis in the future. Especially in operations research, keeping abreast of the new thinking is quite important.

For the next few weeks there was nothing that anyone in the OR department wanted to talk about. Don had said he wasn't going to waste his time or company money on this project any longer, and Gene had told him to stay with it. Don perfunctorily continued to work in the credit area, but they both knew there would be little progress.

In the lunchroom, most of the other analysts sided with Don. They felt that Gene was an opportunist, who was willing to sell them out to the highest bidder and didn't really accept professional standards in handling client problems. In fact, the OR group became more cohesive over this question. Increasingly, the analysts took the position that theirs was a high-level staff group that should work on very advanced corporate problems of long-run significance. More short-run or more mundane problems could be handled by other trouble-shooting departments.

Phase I of the bad-debt model was finally completed, more or less, five months later. In a progress report to his boss, Gene made the following statement at the conclusion of the comments concerning the bad-debt model:

"Phase II of this project will begin at a later date in order to allow the credit department to apply the program developed in Phase I. The feedback from the practical applications will determine the course that future work in this area will take."

In other words, after some eleven months, the bad-debt project was quietly dropped.

Discussion Questions

1. To what extent do you think the lack of acceptance of the OR department was related to the selling orientation of the company? Are there other organizational climates where an OR group would be more acceptable? If so, where, and why?

2. Given Don's unhappiness about the project before he even began it, do you think that Gene should have given him more directives at the beginning? Why, or why not?

3. Reflecting on question two, is there any way to tell

whether Don's failure was simply a self-confirming prophecy on his part? How could you do this?

4. How could Don have handled Cristo in a more productive manner? How would you assess Cristo's role in the organization? Do you think he was being protective? Why would he behave in this way?

5. Assuming that the clash between professional ambitions (such as Don's) and managerial strategy is going to occur, how can the costs of this conflict be minimized?

6. The OR department, as the case ends, has a real problem. What advice would you give Gene on handling the situation? Can it be salvaged? How?

5

the eager new lawyer
and the managing clerk

I was a lawyer with Messrs. Allan and Banes for fifteen years and watched young lawyers come and go. Ours was a large Australian firm, employing 40 staff people. It was also one of the more prestigious firms, having established over the previous fifty years an enviable reputation for reliability and competency. I think the following case will give you some picture of a newcomer's introduction to our firm and to the profession of law.

Messrs. Allan and Banes had a reputation for conservatism, which reflected the influence of the partners, and, to a lesser extent, the nature of the work handled. There were eight partners in the firm: five specialized in corporation work, and the remaining three headed the departments of property, probate (wills and trusts) and common law (court cases such as motor-vehicle collisions).

Although the staff (that is, the nonpartners) numbered approximately 40 people, only about 15 actually handled legal work; the balance comprising girls of various ages who performed secretarial and receptionist duties. These 15 people fell into two categories: those who were qualified attorneys, and those who were not. Those who were unqualified fell into two subcategories termed Managing Clerks and Articled Clerks. The distinction was important, because managing clerks could never advance, whereas articled clerks were generally younger people who had graduated from law school. After graduating it is necessary to work for a year in an attorney's office for the purpose of supplementing the more theoretical law school with some practical experience. At the conclusion

of that year, and after satisfying certain further requirements (examinations, character) the articled clerk is admitted to the practice of law and finally becomes qualified as an attorney.

It was into this somewhat rarified atmosphere that
Jack Bohnston stepped. He was young, eager, fresh from
law school, and bursting with knowledge of the latest
trends in law. In short, he knew a lot about what the law
is, was, and ought to be. Now he was about to apply it.
Nevertheless, Bohnston was not unmindful of the fact
that he was fortunate to be doing his articles with Messrs.
Allan and Banes and that the attorney to whom he was
"articled" was Mr. McLloyd, one of the senior partners
of the firm. McLloyd was in the corporation department.

On his first day, Bohnston was advised by McLloyd
that over a period of time he would be rotated through
each department of the firm. This would enable Bohnston to gain some insight into the main branches of the
law so that he would then be in a better position to assess the merits of each department and decide in which
field to specialize. The first department was to be the
property department; and in view of Mr. McLloyd's busy
schedule, and the fact that he primarily operated in a
different department, Bohnston was advised that he was
to be placed under the control and direction of Mr.
Lawson.

Ned Lawson had been with Messrs. Allan and Banes
for about ten years. He was sixty-three years of age, and
due to retire in two years. Mr. Lawson was English, and
had worked for an English firm of attorneys for some
twenty years. He decided to leave England, and on his
arrival in Australia found employment with Messrs. Allan
and Banes. At no time had Lawson become or attempted
to become an attorney; he was a managing clerk with
considerable experience but no legal qualifications.

The building occupied by the firm was old, with large
rooms and high ceilings. Lawson had one of the largest
offices, and he liked the prestige and the privacy which
accompanied it. He also appreciated the fact that he was
well regarded in the firm because of his considerable practical experience, and that he was assigned a permanent
secretary for his sole convenience.

After Jack Bohnston was shown round the offices of
the firm by the partner in charge of the property department, and introduced to the other partners and staff, he
met Lawson. After the usual introductory remarks, the

property partner remarked to Bohnston that this was the room where he would work for the immediate future, and that in the first instance he was under control of Lawson, then himself, and ultimately Mr. McLloyd.

On that first day, and over the next couple of weeks, a series of events occurred which greatly discouraged Jack Bohnston. These events or incidents were all of a very minor, almost petty nature.

As mentioned, Lawson's office was spacious, and in the middle of the room stood his large desk. Bohnston's desk, situated in a far corner, was more like a tiny table virtually surrounded by Lawson's filing cabinets. In these first days Bohnston required very little secretarial assistance; but when it was necessary, he was authorized by the property partner to use Lawson's secretary. When he did this, he found that the work was seldom returned to him the same day. Bohnston received few telephone calls, and held no conferences. Lawson's telephone rang continually, and he held many conferences. During these conferences Lawson occasionally introduced Bohnston to the firm's client with the comment, "This is the new articled clerk. I'm keeping an eye on him." More often, Bohnston was studiously ignored. Lawson handled a heavy volume of work, and often requested Bohnston to assist him by performing minor and menial tasks. These requests generally came at a time when Bohnston had other work to complete; work assigned to him not only by the property partners but also by the other partners.

Bohnston did not see any particular significance in these assignments. But although he outwardly remained polite and courteous, the appropriate role for the firm's most recent employee, inwardly he was frustrated and disappointed and anxiously awaited the end of the year when his "penal" servitude would end. He felt he was regarded as an idiot, capable only of running errands; his lengthy and specialized training seemed of little use, and he almost had to beg for his work to be typed. He received virtually no recognition, prestige, or status. The work he was given seemed unimportant, but it often required reference to Lawson, an unqualified person anyway, who gave advice in a grudging and abrupt manner if he gave it at all. And when Lawson did pay attention he wanted to chat about his family.

Each of the partners wanted their work to be done immediately, and thus when Bohnston received several matters on one day, he succeeded in satisfying none of the partners. Bohnston could not help comparing his position with that of a close friend who, on graduating from law school, had decided not to do his articles and had gone straight into a corporation. This friend worked shorter hours, received three times Bohnston's salary, had his own office and secretary, not to mention other corporation fringe benefits.

About a month or so after Bohnston had joined Messrs. Allan and Banes, Bohnston approached Lawson about some matter and again was caught in a family-type conversation during which Lawson remarked that as he was approaching retiring age, Bohnston would be the last articled clerk he trained; indeed, he had thought that the previous articled clerk he had trained would be the last.

Pondering Lawson's comments that night, the minor incidents of the first few weeks on the job now took on a new significance. Bohnston began to wonder how he would feel if, at the close of his working years, with age catching up and perhaps his patience and tolerance slowing down, he was asked to train "just one last articled clerk." Bohnston knew how he would feel! Bohnston also knew how he would feel about other matters, such as sharing an office and a secretary.

Along with this new view of Lawson, Bohnston reconsidered his own position. Although there was no question about his legal knowledge and ability, he realized that he was really very ignorant about the procedural aspects of the law. He also realized that this was precisely what Lawson possessed and that McLloyd, in placing him under Lawson, was well aware of Lawson's wealth of experience and hoped that it would be of help to him.

With these new perspectives of Lawson and of himself, Bohnston found everything very different over the next few weeks. He discovered that Lawson usually arrived an hour before the official starting time, and that if he himself also arrived during that hour Lawson was most affable and quite happy to discuss any current matters and to suggest alternative solutions to problems.

Bohnston now appreciated that during working hours Lawson did not have much time to do this. He still assisted Lawson; but Lawson explained not only what was to be done, but also the background of the matter and why it had to be carried out in a certain manner. Lawson provided Bohnston with technical aid and also gave him personal support. Occasionally a matter of Bohnston's did not develop as it should have, and if Bohnston had previously discussed it with Lawson, then Lawson would also attend the meeting with the property partner and would support Bohnston in the action he took and elaborate on the reasons. When the quantity of work that Bohnston handled increased, Lawson supported Bohnston's application for more secretarial assistance.

Thus Bohnston's attitude toward Lawson and the firm changed completely, but two matters still caused him some concern. The first arose from the fact that he still felt relatively deprived as compared with his close friend who was employed by a corporation. The second matter that caused him concern arose from the fact that, notwithstanding the clear chain of command indicated to him at the outset, none of the partners observed this and he continued to receive work from them all. He really was not sure whose directives were to be followed or in what order.

Discussion Questions

1. Comment on Bohnston's job expectations as a recently trained "professional," and how consistent they were with the realities of organization life and the needs of this particular firm. Do you think professional training should be more reality oriented? How?

2. Was Lawson a good choice to supervise Bohnston? How much supervision, and of what kind, was Bohnston prepared to accept? Was he realistic? Explain.

3. Do you think that professionally educated individuals are difficult to train on the job? Why, or why not?

4. What explains the dramatic change in Lawson's behavior vis-à-vis Bohnston? Does this seem realistic under the circumstances?

5. What do you think could have been done to insure Bohnston's "seeing the light" earlier?

6. What does the case illustrate concerning the professional's "trade-off" of money versus status or training?

7. Why is someone of marginal status more likely to resent "unprofessional" work, than a colleague with a higher status?

8. How would you assess the management structure of Messrs. Allan and Banes? Do you think the organization is well run? Why, or why not?

6

a change in
the editorial department

Jackson Company is a small New York City publisher. The company produces a monthly technical magazine aimed at approximately 28,000 design engineers who receive the magazine free of charge. In other words, the circulation is controlled and fixed. This magazine required the coordination of personnel in advertising, sales, research, promotion, circulation, and editing. Because the magazine is distributed free, advertising provides all revenue. Our main concern will be with the activities of the editorial department.

The general atmosphere which prevailed in the editorial department was one of informality and casualness. There was considerable freedom from formal controls despite the monthly deadline dates for completion of manuscripts. Each of the nine editors was a highly skilled engineer-writer with extensive specialized experience in one or more distinct fields of engineering. Aside from editing and revising articles received from outside authors, a good deal of original work was done by individual editors.

Top management recognition of the editors' technical superiority and encouragement of their individual abilities resulted in their preferential treatment—freedom of movement, choice offices, individual secretaries—which enhanced their feeling of superiority and set the editorial group apart from the rest of the company. Interaction with the other departments was kept at a minimum. Within the small editorial group, however, there was considerable solidarity and cooperation, and the nature of their duties required continuous interaction.

The editor-in-chief, Alistair King, solicited, accepted or rejected articles from outside authors, coordinated and directly supervised his department, revised manuscripts, scheduled and allocated work among his editors, and performed other administrative tasks. No systematic method of planned scheduling or follow-up of written material had been devised to handle the flow of work in and out of the department. Deadlines were frequently ignored, monthly issues of the magazine were consistently coming out late, complaints were received from the readers, advertisers, company salesmen, and other departments in which work had been delayed. The editorial department, for the most part, ignored these complaints.

In order to correct this situation, an editorial programmer, Douglas Niles, was hired to serve as the right-hand man to King. Niles's duties were to relieve King and the technical editors of production scheduling details and routines. He was to supervise the editorial production section, and to have overall supervision of the editorial secretaries as a group; reporting absences, tardiness, and general deportment of the secretaries directly to the personnel department. However, it was made clear to the editors at the beginning that the new programmer was not to supervise them but to work with them in facilitating the flow of copy to production. He would have no authority to issue orders to them; suggestions and proposed changes in methods or procedures would be presented to the editor-in-chief, and all instructions would be issued only through Mr. King.

A systematic routing and scheduling procedure was devised. A schedule board of articles, dates, and names of editors was set up to show the stage of progress of each article. Editors were required to report proposed field trips well in advance, and keep Niles informed as to manuscript progress. Copyreading for style uniformity; checking dummy pages, galleys, and page proofs; issuing reminders to editors on due dates for copy; and maintenance of editor production records were some of the additional duties of Doug Niles.

Briefly, the procedure worked something like this: An article came in from an author and was accepted by King. The manuscript was passed to Niles, who recorded it and assigned it to a particular editor. Manuscript and art work were then edited and returned to Niles, who read them for uniformity of style and then either returned them to the editor for revision or sent them to King for checking and approval. The manuscript was then returned to Niles who expedited it through production, checked dummies, page proofs, and art work, and then released it to the printers.

In September and October, the first two months following the installation of the new system, no appreciable change in work-flow speed was evident. The magazine was still being held up on account of late manuscripts and other difficulties. But after Niles had oriented the editors in the procedures, and had had a chance to put the new system into operation, the editors found that a good part of their routine work was being relieved and they were able to concentrate on the more important aspects of their jobs. They found themselves able to handle their work more efficiently and without sacrificing good quality standards. Therefore, in November, December, and January, the magazine came out on the first day of each month, or even one or two days before the first. In February, however, and in subsequent months, a reversion to the old pattern of lateness and overstepped deadlines took place and persisted despite the heroic efforts of Niles to correct the situation.

Management was baffled by this latest turn of events. No one seemed able to pinpoint the problem.

Discussion Questions

1. Does the fact that the magazine has a controlled circulation and free distribution affect the operations of the editorial department? How? Would a conventionally distributed magazine have a different editorial operation? Why?

2. Examine the professionalism which existed in the editorial department prior to the introduction of the editorial programmer Doug Niles. In what way did this hinder or help the operations of the department?

3. Why do you think operations were so inefficient in the editorial department before the change? What was really happening?

4. What are the typical examples of resistance to

change in an organization? Did you see anything similar happening in the editorial department when Niles was brought in? Discuss.

5. Do you think the introduction of Niles was the best change that management could have made? Why, or why not? What other changes could have been made?

6. After a couple of months, the introduction of Niles appeared to be paying dividends—operations were more efficient, the magazine was meeting its deadlines, et cetera. But just when operations were running smoothly, a reversion to the old patterns of inefficiency took place. What would be some possible reasons for this? Discuss.

7. As our case ends, the situation at the Jackson Company appears no better than when it began. You can imagine that management would be pretty desperate by now. Assume that they have hired you as a consultant to aid them in solving the problems in their editorial department. What would you recommend? Be certain that your recommendations are feasible.

7

bad times
come to hanesville

I am employed by Spitz Merchandise, Inc., as a truck driver. My job is a simple one, consisting of driving a shuttle truck between the factory in Crestwood and the warehouse in Hanesville, New Jersey, a distance of approximately ten miles. I have developed close contacts with the warehouse crew, for I spend a major portion of my time there helping to load and unload trucks between runs. Let me tell you about some of the things that have recently happened there.

Consisting of a small crew, a secretary, and a foreman, the warehouse in Hanesville held a rather unique position in the Spitz Merchandise organization. Aside from a slightly higher pay scale, the warehousemen enjoyed having their own "shop." The six warehousemen were black; five were native Americans, and one was from Cuba. The Cuban, however, had come to this country at an early age and Spanish was not his first language. Their names were Al, Donald, Eddy, Frank, Billy, and Mingo. All used handjacks (hydraulic hand-pulled devices used to transport merchandise on wooden pallets) except for Al, who drove a forklift. Vicki, the secretary, played only a minor role in the warehouse operation. The foreman Angelo was Italian, and had worked for the firm for over twenty years. He was considered the company's best foreman, and because of this he was entrusted with managing the warehouse. His supervisor was the plant manager in the nearby city of Crestwood; Angelo, however, wasn't afraid to go to the president of the firm when he had a problem.

The warehousemen received daily instructions from

Angelo; these consisted of assigning which orders were to be "pulled," and who was to help load which trucks. Depending on the number of orders shipped, Al and one or two of the other men would work in the back of the warehouse at the receiving docks helping me unload merchandise arriving from Crestwood.

Angelo poked fun at the inept people over in Crestwood and enjoyed the Hanesville location for it allowed him to "run a tight ship." Angelo was a most popular man, and, although a demanding foreman, he had the complete respect of his crew. This popularity was partially attributable to his nature; but, more importantly, Angelo knew how to plan work so that there were few crises which required pushing his men.

When a new man joined the crew he was accepted only after proving to them that he was not a "goof-off." Also, members of the crew were expected to limit themselves to one soda in the morning and one in the afternoon. Violations of this rule, or taking of extra soda breaks was justification for a "pop" in the belly and the title of "Soda Man." It also was an expected part of the job that the men would help in the back when necessary, although shipping was considered more important by the men.

Angelo was aware of this cohesion, as was upper management, and thus remained selective in his personnel practices even when short of men. He also emphasized the importance of shipping, and praised his men generously in front of upper management. Angelo was able to prevent any "bad apples" from spoiling his crew by firing any newcomers who did not meet his high standards. This was a distinction among Spitz foremen, for low pay schedules usually necessitated the keeping of all hired personnel. Angelo's policy served as a source of pride to the men who remained at the warehouse.

Al was probably the most amicable member of the crew, but his position as forklift operator kept him in the receiving area; and although in contact with the others, he did not assume leadership of the group. Mingo, the smallest man, was the best worker and became the group's informal leader. Mingo could best be described as a hustler, always doing more than his share and helping out whenever any of the others fell behind. In addition, Mingo felt the closest attachment to the company and especially to "his warehouse."

After only two years of existence the Hanesville warehouse was considered the smoothest operation in the work flow. Other areas showed fluctuations in output, but this warehouse could be counted on to meet its quota even during the height of the shipping season in early fall.

Spitz is a manufacturer of garment accessories (hangers, shoe racks, and tie racks) and most of their products are in wire, tubing, and plastics. The company introduced "dressing valets" to its line in early 1967, and a new department was created to handle assembly of this item. The valets were an immediate success, and soon the department outgrew its allocated space in Crestwood. It was then decided to transfer the assembly and packaging operation to Hanesville, and production and plating would remain in Crestwood.

General confusion prevailed in the back of the warehouse as the valet operation took shape. Storage space became cramped as more room was needed, and added pressure was placed on Al, myself, and the other men who now had to unload unfinished valets in addition to the other merchandise.

The valet crew was all Puerto Rican and consisted of two men and five women. They were all new workers, and were paid the minimum wage. Under Tony's supervision, a newly appointed foreman who previously was a welder, the crew was inefficient and unconcerned with their work. They kept apart from the warehouse crew, and even stayed in the rear of the building during coffee and lunch breaks. (The warehouse crew had always taken their breaks either outdoors or on the loading docks near the coffee truck.)

As the weeks passed, valet assembly failed to meet quotas and problems arose in coordinating valet production with assembly and packaging. Management considered transfer of the operation, but lack of space at Crestwood and the already begun fall season prevented such action.

As valet production and assembly fell behind, men from the shipping department alternated in helping Al and me unload the trucks. This job became a source of discomfort for the warehousemen and also became a distasteful task for it involved not only leaving the ordered and efficient atmosphere Angelo commanded for the "mess back there" but it meant working with the strangers. In an effort to remedy the situation, Mingo was sent to the receiving department—much to his displeasure; but the problem still remained.

For the first time since moving to Hanesville, the shipping department failed to meet its quota in July. In addition, the men began complaining of the heat, though previously everyone used to say that this was the coolest of the company's warehouses. The men complained of cramped quarters, but made little effort to straighten out the growing disorder which had spread to their department. Angelo, although aware of the problem, was unable to get his men to straighten things out because they blamed the valet department for the mess.

Discontentment spread, and an increasing number of orders was being misplaced or incorrectly filled, and merchandise was damaged during unloading. In what seems to have been the breaking point in the conflict, one of the men in the valet crew was allowed to play his radio and kept it loudly tuned to a Spanish station. This was a special source of aggravation to Eddy, who had been told by Angelo that he could not have a radio at work. Eddy quit three days later. Finally Mingo, who had shown great displeasure at the valet crew's sloppiness and poor production, became irritated when addressed in Spanish by the valet crew and got in a fight with Frank when he (Frank) misplaced an order. As a result, Mingo was fired.

The warehousemen came to view the warehouse as a sloppy place in which to work, blaming the problem on the valet crew. It became difficult for Angelo to get his men to help out in the receiving area or keep order up front. The growing resentment of the warehousemen was evidenced by their half-hearted attempts to keep the shipping area in order as they complained of conditions. Eventually the group found the "heat" a problem, and one day tempers flared and a fight broke out between the men.

The situation grew worse until Angelo went to the president and demanded that the valets go—or he would. The president, aware of the situation, was able to assure Angelo that after the season was over the valet department would be moved. Shipping levels then ended their new declining trend, but remained low and erratic for many months.

Order was finally restored the following year, after the valet assembly was moved to its own location; however, of the original crew only one man remained. Never again did the Hanesville warehouse enjoy its former enviable position in the organization.

Discussion Questions

1. *In what way does the case suggest that effective supervision (creating high morale and cohesiveness) can occur only with isolation of the work group? Do you agree with this contention? Why, or why not?*

2. *How can a supervisor ameliorate ethnic or racial rivalries? Does Angelo's fostering of a group spirit make the situation worse, or better? Explain your answer.*

3. *How realistic is it for a manager to expect to have a homogeneous (in terms of backgrounds and interests) group of subordinates who will become a tightly knitted "clique"? Should management encourage this because it makes supervision easier? Is there anything negative about such homogeneity?*

4. *How much would the situation have been improved if the work flow problems of valet assembly—extending back to Crestwood—had been solved by upper management? What do you think of the management at Spitz?*

5. *Explain why the radio became a symbol. Can you think of similar symbols in your own work experiences?*

6. *Is it likely that the work problems were compounded by the Puerto Rican employees' knowledge of the resentment of the other workers? What is the likely effect of their having a foreman who could not speak their language? Compare their likely attitudes with those of the more senior group, the black men.*

7. *Would greater isolation of the two groups have helped—if this could have been accomplished by relocating some of the operations in the warehouse? Discuss.*

8

conflict at sea

This case involved a naval ship which I shall call the USS Problem. This ship was used to launch and fly radio-controlled planes as targets for fleet gunnery practice and as part of the guided-missile program of the Navy and the Air Force, and was commanded by Lieutenant Jackson. The executive officer was Lieutenant Junior Grade Myles. The remainder of the ship's company consisted of four ensigns—Lawson, Randolph, Greer, and Smathers, plus a crew of 60 enlisted men. The enlisted men were divided into the normal divisions of a ship: engineering, deck operations, supply and medical. The entire duty of this crew of six officers and 60 men involved running the ship. They did not fly, maintain, or prepare the planes. These particular operations were carried out by Utility Squadron 81, made up of 12 enlisted men who were in the Naval Air Force, and Lieutenant Crane, the officer in charge.

While the men of Utility Squadron 81 were aboard, they did in fact become members of the crew of the ship and were designated the Air Division. They worked and stood watches on the ship as did the rest of the crew. Navy regulations state that the captain and the executive officer—in this case Lieutenant Jackson, and Lieutenant (JG) Myles, respectively—are always senior and in command of any officers assigned to the ship, no matter what their rank. Regulations further state that whereas any officer must "go through" the executive officer before bringing any matter to the captain, if the officer is senior in rank to the executive officer, he may go directly to the captain. Therefore, in this present case, Lieutenant Crane could report directly to Lieutenant Jackson without first having to see Lieutenant Myles.

This year, when the new air group reported aboard, relations between this group and the remainder of the crew were harmonious and cooperative. But within a few short months Lieutenant Crane was heard to mutter about the incompetency of Lieutenant Myles, the executive officer. These remarks were usually made to the four ensigns or to the enlisted men of the air group—but never to Lieutenant Myles, or to Lieutenant Jackson.

On the other side of the picture, Lieutenant Myles said little about Lieutenant Crane but seemed to take extraordinary pains to detect any mistakes made by the air group. The nature of the air group's work often required that prior to or after air operations the men of the group had to be excused from regular watches, or special provisions had to be made for feeding the men at odd hours. These concessions, although they were necessary, were given somewhat grudgingly by Lieutenant Myles. During this period of time, the four ensigns became good friends with Lieutenant Crane, and were soon heard to be complaining under their breath about the executive officer.

Relationships between the remainder of the ship's company and the air group deteriorated as the year progressed. Complaints were often heard about the privileges of the airmen (odd eating hours, priority in chow lines, permission to skip watches, et cetera). The ship's company also accused the airmen of being sloppy in manner and appearance as well as stuffy because they did not associate with the rest of the crew.

The airmen, on their part, claimed that the ship's company was too regulation-conscious and so busy doing inane work that they couldn't appreciate the importance of the work of the airmen. The airmen felt that much of the complaining of the ship's company was "sour grapes." As a result of these feelings, the airmen were just as happy to be left alone by the rest of the crew. They kept to themselves, and even refused to go to the parties given on the ship (in which the rest of the crew participated). Feelings ran so high that fist fights between members of the air group and the ship's company became almost a daily occurrence. As the year progressed, matters did not improve. The effectiveness of the ship was greatly reduced.

The solution of the problem was simply the replacement of the air group at the end of their year tour of duty. Unfortunately, past experience has shown that the same thing could happen all over again with the new airmen. The Navy is quite distressed by this continuing conflict, and since these ships are needed and can be staffed only by a combination of ship's company and airmen, the officials in charge are somewhat at a loss as to what can be done.

Discussion Questions

1. It appears that there was a rather serious conflict between the officer in charge of the airmen, Lieutenant Crane, and Executive Officer Lieutenant JG Myles. What do you think caused this conflict? Do you think it was a personality problem? Why, or why not?

2. Analyze the reactions of the two major groups in this case—the airmen and the ship's company. What do you think was the basic cause of their animosity toward each other?

3. Assume that you were assigned by the Navy to investigate this situation. Given the information you have, indicate the following:

(a) What you think the basic problems are.

(b) What recommendations you would make to improve the situation.

(c) The types of resistance you would face by the various individuals or groups involved.

(d) What you would do to overcome this resistance.

9

the luggers
versus the butchers

Food Merchandising Corporation had one of its warehouses in a small city in Northern New Jersey. The main operation of the warehouse was to stock certain goods, and then ship them on order to various stores. The meat department handled packaged meats, and wholesale cuts of lamb, veal, and beef. Beef, by far the biggest and most expensive commodity, was generally bought from midwestern packers and shipped either by railroad or truck. On arrival at the warehouse, the beef was in the form of two hindquarters and two forequarters, each weighing close to two hundred pounds. The problem was to get these heavy pieces of meat off the trucks (or freight cars) and onto the intricate system of rails within the warehouse. Freight was paid by the shipper.

Company and union rules proscribed warehousemen from unloading trucks. It became the function of the general warehouseman (designated "lugger") to assist in the unloading of the trucks, but with no lifting. If, however, the beef was shipped by rail, it became his function to unload the freight cars. After the meat was placed on company rails, it was pushed through the doors into the 35° warehouse where it was placed in stock until it was butchered. The butchery process involved several men. First, the meat went to the sawman. While someone steadied the meat on the rail, the rib, plate, brisket, and shoulder bones were severed. Then it was passed on to the cutters, who butchered it into several smaller wholesale cuts. After that the meat was again placed in stock to be shipped out by the night crews.

THE "LUGGERS" VERSUS THE "BUTCHERS"

The operation of the warehouse involved two distinct functions: to unload and stock the beef, and then to butcher it. The unloading process was wholly different from the butchering. It required physical strength and coordination to lift 200 pounds of beef all day. Furthermore, when the workload slowed down, the luggers were given different tasks. There was a degree of variety in their work. But the butchering function was very different. The men were geographically confined to the cutting line and performed the same basic operations day after day.

When the warehouse was unionized eight years ago, the men who had most seniority were given first option as to the jobs they preferred. Since many of these men were on the older side, they gravitated away from the more laborious general warehouse work toward the higher-wage butcher jobs. Consequently, two different types of individuals became associated with the two different types of jobs.

The eight butchers were engaged in the skilled practice of butchering meat. Most of them had been with the company for many years. For the most part, they were family men with many off-the-job responsibilities, were by no means in union affairs, and probably had more loyalty to the company than to the union local. They had a high number of social activities off-the-job such as group picnics, bowling, golf, et cetera. The tedious boredom of their job was somewhat mitigated by these mutual activities, and an atmosphere of good humor usually prevailed in their corner of the warehouse.

There were nine luggers, but two of these had been butchers until very recently. More will be said later about these men. A third man usually worked in another section. Thus the term "lugger" referred to a specific group of six general warehousemen. These men were younger and generally had less company time than the butchers, but this is not to say that they were young or new. Most of them were married, but treated their home responsibilities differently. For instance, the typical butcher would spend his night at home, and most of the luggers would spend their night working a part-time job.

HANK, JOSH, AND MR. ABRAMS

Hank was the foreman. When he became foreman about ten years ago, the men considered him a walking terror but a good foreman. Now he was considered neither. There were several reasons for this change. First, the coming of the union had made Hank more careful in the way he handled the men. Second, Hank had lost control of the luggers. After several fiery confrontations, he more or less left them alone. When it was necessary to give them an order, great explanations and apologies often accompanied it. His relationship with butchers, however, remained fairly intact. In effect, Hank was afraid of the luggers but not of the butchers. Third, when Mr. Abrams became manager two years ago it was his policy to use close personal supervision of the men to insure efficiency. Mr. Abrams, therefore, usurped considerable portions of Hank's responsibility.

Josh was the union representative. He had built up a great friendship with Carl, the shop steward, and the other luggers. His relationship with the butchers, however, was strictly on a business basis. As a consequence, Josh tended to favor the luggers in any controversy. Usually this meant that the butchers complained about the luggers, but nothing really important was done about it.

Mr. Abrams' assistant was Lyle, nicknamed "the Puppy." Lyle used to follow Mr. Abrams everywhere he went, to the great enjoyment of the men. Thus came the nickname "Puppy."

The butchers took the brunt of Mr. Abrams' close supervision, mainly because they were confined to one spot and were easy to observe. Also, this was where the real pressure had to be applied; for if the meat was not butchered, it could not be sent out and stores would run short. Mr. Abrams had the responsibility to ensure that stores were not short. He evidently felt that standing over the men (with the Puppy at his side) would cut down on the little games the men developed to break up their boring routine (talking, bathroom breaks, et cetera). The net effect was that the men, being oldtimers, took their breaks anyway but grumbled about being watched over. The luggers were harder to watch, being more spread out, and they also managed to gain some control over Mr. Abrams. He knew that an ill-timed remark or too much supervision would only result in later slowdowns by these men.

A SLOW CHANGE IN STATUS

Six years ago the butcher's job was considered much more desirable than that of the luggers. At that time most of the meat was shipped by railroad. This necessitated a great deal of heavy work. Most of the men would have preferred the cold monotony of cutting meat to lugging 200 pounds of beef from a railroad car to a loading dock. It was at this point that two luggers, Brent and Terry, began to think of developing a system of portable rails that would be adaptable to the large variety of freight cars which came to the warehouse. The rails were successfully designed and developed by the two men. With the passage of time, skill in their use was achieved and the job of unloading freight cars became quite simple.

The ingenuity of two luggers was widely heralded about the warehouse and in the company, and recognition was given in due proportion. More importantly, a job that was undesirable before became quite attractive because the chief reason for its undesirability had ceased to exist. The main attractions of the butcher's job were reduced to the companionship of the group, the waning prestige of being a skilled workman, and the higher-wage-more-overtime benefits. This was quite sufficient to keep them satisfied, if not as happy as before.

Hank's foremanship also suffered. At this date, his position had already been dealt a few blows by the union and the men. Now an innovation was introduced that had no place in his way of doing things. He preferred to completely ignore the rails and allow the luggers to use them as they saw fit. From the company's point of view, the use of rails in freight cars meant very little. Four men were still required in each car. Efficiency remained about the same because it took time to assemble and disassemble the rail system.

If the use of the rails had resulted solely in physical advantages, it is probable that the situation would have gone along unchanged. But the luggers were quick to discover an economic value in their use. The trucks coming in on the front docks had to be unloaded. Since freight was paid by the shipper, the company and union had worked out an agreement in which the trucker was responsible for delivering the meat to the dock. The warehouse workers were only to assist peripherally, and were not permitted inside the trucks unless it was absolutely necessary.

The drivers were not happy with their lot of unloading up to 35,000 pounds of beef. Consequently, they often hired warehouse vagrants—men who sat around the warehouse waiting for such opportunities. The going rate was one dollar per 1,000 pounds: between $30.00 and $35.00 a truck. It generally took two hours to unload one truck. The enterprising luggers redesigned the rails for use on the trucks, and made it known that a tip of two dollars was in order for anyone who cared to use them. Since the railroad was making more and more use of piggyback services, the number of trucks as well as the amount of the tips began to increase.

A DISPUTE DEVELOPS

Last year, two butchers were given the option of working as luggers. They exercised the option, partly hoping to recuperate some of their wage losses by sharing in the tip money. It was not long before serious arguments developed between the old and new luggers. Beforehand, the luggers had worked out a one-for-you and one-for-me system with the trucks. Such an informal understanding was possible because this tightly cohesive group knew that petty bickering would soon take the problem out of their own hands. The two ex-butchers, however, had no desire to work with the old group. They were in no way amenable to tacit understandings that cut them out. Consequently, when the big trailers turned into the driveway, there began a jockeying for position.

Arguments developed, and other work suffered. When the two ex-butchers turned to the union, they found their upward paths of communication thoroughly blocked. Carl, the shop steward, was a lugger. It was to his disadvantage to press hard on behalf of the two ex-butchers. Josh, the union representative, was much too friendly with the luggers and no progress could be made here. Hank, the foreman, was worthless in this matter; and Mr. Abrams was too new at this stage to take action. For these reasons, and because of a normal reluctance to push grievances, little pressure was placed on the union.

Early last spring, following a series of flare-ups over equipment usage and truck tips, two "clubs" were formed: Club "Six" and Club "Three." Brent, one of the two rail designers, originated the idea of formalizing the two groups. Each club was given a separate locker for equipment. No exchanges were to take place. Members of Club Three (the two ex-butchers and a third who worked in a different part of the warehouse) were permitted to work a share of trucks proportional to club membership. Members of Club Six (the six original luggers) began a practice of pooling tips and dividing them equally.

At first the formalization of the two groups appeared to be a good solution. There were fewer arguments, and Club Three was reasonably satisfied. However, an unfortunate side effect developed. Previously, the distinctions between luggers and butchers were implicit and the warehouse as a whole was a friendly place. People knew who got along with whom, and friendships often crossed group lines. With the formalization, however, people began to class themselves as "in" or "out." Club Six members began to be more and more isolated among the 25 men who worked in this section of the warehouse. Butchers and luggers constantly complained about each other. Members of Club Six refused to work with members of Club Three, and much ill feeling was generated. But even so, had there been nothing else, these difficulties would probably not have caused any lasting problems. There was, however, something else—the piggyback development.

The railroads were making more and more use of piggyback trucking. This is a system whereby trailers are hauled part of the way by rail, and part of the way by road. As the number of freight cars decreased and the warehouse volume increased, more trucks began coming. These trucks had to be unloaded, and unloading was an expensive and time-consuming proposition. The use of rails on the trucks had cut down the time it took to unload. A good crew could "knock one off" in less than an hour, though the average time was about two hours. The luggers began to move into this very lucrative area. It became quite a steady thing for them to bring home an extra $30.00 or $40.00 per week. Occasionally, if things were slow enough, the luggers would work a truck on company time. Or they would begin setting it up about 3:30, so there would be no delay in getting it started at 4:00.

From the company viewpoint, there was no problem. Trucks were being emptied faster than ever before, even on the rare occasion when a truck came in purposely late. The more usual situation was either that there were too many trucks to unload in the normal day or that the truck was legitimately delayed. At any rate, the rails enabled the ordinary trucks to be unloaded much more rapidly and the experienced luggers often finished their after-hour trucks in half the normal time. Warehouse efficiency did not suffer.

The butchers, however, were not a happy group. They continued to work the same boring routine in the same 35°. Their income did not change. They watched the luggers develop into a very cohesive group, and usurped their status position. They resented the different treatments meted out to the two groups. The luggers were given too much freedom, and the butchers were too closely supervised. The luggers quite often "couldn't" stay overtime, yet they could almost always work a truck. Nothing was ever said when luggers made excuses; but if the butchers did not want to stay, they were given a great deal of grief.

Pressure was applied, and it was not a rare thing to find butchers working three hours overtime for half the money the luggers made in an hour by working a truck. The obvious inequity was deeply resented. The luggers used company time to work trucks, or to set them up, and this violated the union contract. Yet nothing concrete was ever done to stop them. The butchers felt totally frustrated and disenchanted with what they had once considered as high-status jobs. Despite their innate conservatism and procompany attitude they seriously considered a massive walkout to get their grievances heard.

Discussion Questions

1. *As operations change, status of various groups is often affected. In what way has the status of the luggers and butchers changed over the years?*

2. *Describe the work flow at Food Merchandising Corporation. Do you think it is efficient? Why? Describe any way in which you think it could be improved.*

3. *Show how membership in the various groups de-*

scribed affected behavior. Do you think that management effectively utilized the natural formation of these groups to the betterment of operations? Explain.

4. *How did the various technological changes in the meat-packing industry affect operations at Food Merchandising? How did the various groups—luggers, butchers, and management—react to these changes?*

5. *Analyze Mr. Abrams' style of supervision. What effect did this have on the relationships between the luggers and the butchers?*

6. *What is your view of Brent and Terry? Are they beneficial to the operations of the company, or not? Explain. How would you deal with these two men?*

7. *Analyze the dispute that led to the formation of Club Six and Club Three. In what ways were the formation of these "clubs" beneficial or detrimental to the operations of the company? If you were a member of management, how would you have dealt with these two clubs?*

8. *As the case ends, the butchers are threatening a walkout. Can anything be done to avert this? If so, what?*

9. *In assessing the case, what do you think really led to all the problems, i.e., who was at fault? Justify your answers.*

10

the machinists

In October 1966, construction began on a new can manufacturing plant that was to be ready for production in June 1967. Starting in December 1966, eight machinists and five other mechanics were hired over a period of five months and sent to various eastern and midwestern plants for training. As a group they were considered above average in intelligence and craftsmanship, and performed superior work in the plants they visited.

By late spring of 1967, it became apparent that construction difficulties would force the postponement of the plant opening until the early fall. As a result of this delay, management decided to recall all the men from field training in late June and early July. The reasoning behind this move was that excessive training costs would be eliminated, machine training could be provided locally, and management would have an opportunity to observe their men at firsthand.

Although the new manufacturing plant was not completed, a large temporary warehouse on the premises was in operation. There was considerable work at the warehouse, mainly consisting of unloading and trucking cartons of cans from freight cars and truck trailers into the warehouse, and loading other trucks with cartons of cans for shipment to local customers. Management intended to use the returning trainees for part-time labor in the warehouse during the periods they were not attending equipment school.

When the first group of seven men arrived they were put to work in the warehouse under the direction of the foreman.

From the onset, the shipping foreman was dissatisfied

with the work of the machinists. Some were put in box-cars to unload cartons. Others were put to work inspecting cans. Mr. Yarby, the foreman, later indicated his impression of the machinists.

"I noticed the machinists dogging it. I didn't say anything, because I knew it wasn't their type of work. I didn't mind if they worked slowly, if only they would work steadily."

However, Lars Nelson, a spokesman for the machinists, saw it differently. "We were all slightly shocked that we had to go to the boxcars. We griped, but we did the work."

The superintendent, Dale Karlson, made the following comments on the work of a few machinists who were inspecting cans, which was the most monotonous job in the warehouse. "It seemed to me they weren't doing the same job as the other machinists. They didn't have their hearts in it. I had built up resentment against some of the men from what the foreman told me about them. I didn't speak to any of them about it, however, because I feel that a guy should have only one boss. I heard they were giving the foreman smart answers."

After a week of working in the warehouse, four of the machinists were assigned to equipment school for half of each working day. During the remaining time they were kept on their regular warehouse assignments. Their performance in school was good, but in the warehouse it continued to be poor.

Two weeks later, six other machinist trainees returned to the plant. Their working days were also divided between school and the warehouse. They were put with the shipping personnel so they could get an idea of what was involved in the work.

In school, the men were divided into three groups and given very little supervision. They first received job instructor training with instructors chosen from the group. The equipment they worked on was new, and they had the responsibility for developing written instructions for the operation of each machine. There was considerable group participation, and the men were enthusiastic.

When the new group of six men reported for work, the personnel supervisor told them to come in about an hour late so that the foreman would have a chance to get his department running.

As Nelson put it, "Some of the men came in late for

work because the personnel supervisor asked them to. A few days later, during morning roll call, the foreman mentioned this fact that the men came in late and asked —Who's supposed to pay you guys for that time? The personnel department better pay for it—as if there was a dividing line between shipping and maintenance men. He talked as if the money was coming out of his own pocket."

In the days that followed the machinists began returning late from morning and afternoon breaks. Nelson quoted Yarby's comments on this practice.

"My men get back from breaks on time so why can't you." But according to Nelson, "He (the foreman) always made that distinction between his men and us."

Because of scheduling difficulties, it was sometimes necessary to put three men in a boxcar instead of two.

Yarby: "I saw three men doing the work of one man. I told them it was a one-man job. Perhaps I was a little sarcastic when I said it. It's a bad idea to have them working in groups."

Nelson: "We used to take pride in emptying the cars in about five hours. We kept on making a target for ourselves. When you work together, it isn't so boring because you can talk and work at the same time."

Yarby: "My men started making cracks about the maintenance men. They would say—Look at them (the machinists). I guess it's going to take a couple of days for them to unload that car."

Some of the machinists were unloading cartons of cans from the boxcars. The cartons could not be handled roughly because of danger of damaging the cans.

Yarby: "The men were tossing the cartons. I told them —Don't toss the cartons, just place them. I came back fifteen minutes later, and they were doing the same thing. This time I gave them a direct order and said that I wasn't kidding. I guess I had a nasty look on my face, and I meant it. It was indicative of the type of work they were doing."

Nelson: "There was a big space between the dock and the RR car. It was dangerous to keep walking across the space. We figured out a way of making a sort of fire line and handing the cartons out easier and faster than we could do the regular way. It was also safer because we didn't have to walk across that space. Yarby said we were throwing the cartons, but we really weren't. He made us go back to the old way, and we couldn't understand why."

Another incident that occurred while sorting cans was the following:

Yarby: "I saw a man reading a book about the definition of work. I told him—Let's not read about work but let's get the work done."

Nelson: "We were doing our work at a regular pace and were talking about work. We started to talk about the definition of work, and one of the guys opened his toolbox to look in his physics book for a definition. Just then the foreman came along, and took the guy that had the book and put him to work in another area."

Although not involving Nelson, the following incident is mentioned because it more fully describes the sentiments of some of the men.

A mechanic, Roy Swanson, was put on the job of gluing carton flaps. He had set up a table next to him so that he could read a training manual while he worked. The foreman discovered him.

Yarby: " 'Hey'," I said, " 'if you want to read a manual, I'll charge your time to the training department.' The guy made some answer, but I didn't hear it. It didn't seem nasty or anything."

Swanson: "I kept on thinking I could be doing something else also because it (gluing cartons) didn't require any mental ability and it was driving me nuts. I felt much better after I got my book because I was doing something interesting. I didn't think it interfered with work, because if it did I wouldn't have read. I really think I did more because now I could work more steadily. Otherwise I would have walked around a lot and stalled. The foreman came by and said he could charge my time to training. I didn't say anything. I always had the impression that he disliked maintainers, especially like during roll call when he always says for maintainers to start maintaining or maintainers go to the maintaining area.

"Deep down I guess I knew it wasn't exactly right to have a book out, but I felt I was still doing my work. I felt it should be allowed because it wasn't my regular work, and as long as I was getting it out it was all right."

The men kept returning late from their relief periods, and the foreman cautioned them a number of times. This incident occurred near the end of a relief period.

Nelson: "Everyone had been talking and making remarks about getting back on time for the breaks. I half kiddingly and half seriously said to the guys, 'O.K., men, let's not be staying here. Let's get back on time.' The foreman was standing right near me, and I didn't even know it. He said, 'Yeah, you men look too comfortable.' I think this was the first indication he had that there was dissension among the men."

Soon after this last incident the foreman asked the superintendent to have a meeting with the machinists and mechanics to try to straighten out the situation—which was steadily getting worse. Yarby felt that the men should be informed that present circumstances were due to construction delays, and how this made it necessary for them to perform duties that would otherwise not be theirs.

In preparing for this meeting, Mr. Karlson made the following comment:

"I am glad I am finally going to get a chance to talk directly to this Nelson character. From what I have learned from the foreman, plus what I have seen in my walks through the plant, this guy certainly seems to be a ringleader of this little group—and a troublemaker to boot. I think it might be best to get rid of him. I have the feeling that all these guys of Nelson's think that this work is just a picnic. We will just have to change that notion! They are either going to work properly, or get out."

The meeting was held between the machinists, mechanics, and Karlson. Yarby was intentionally left out of it. After telling the men about the unusual circumstances which resulted in their work situation in the warehouse, Karlson asked them if there was anything on their minds that they would like to discuss. Nelson was the first and most outspoken critic in his condemnation of the foreman. He started with the complaint that Yarby never even said good morning to the men, and ran through most of the other opinions expressed above. The rest of the group wholeheartedly supported Nelson. The superintendent was quite taken aback by some of the complaints.

After the meeting he said, "Boy, that was quite a session. Maybe these guys have something worth complaining about after all. I am not so sure now that Nelson is such a troublemaker—although it is obvious that the men follow his lead. I am going to have to do some more investigation of this. I had better talk with the foreman more closely."

Shortly after all this, a lengthy meeting was held between Karlson, Yarby, and the personnel supervisor of the plant. The foregoing situation was discussed, and the decision was made that it would be best for all concerned if the machinists were taken off their jobs in the warehouse and put in school for full days or at least for as long as possible.

After this meeting, but before the actual move to all-day training, the following two incidents took place:

Yarby: "I noticed cigarettes lying on the pallets a few times. I told them not to smoke in the boxcars. I think they were smoking a good part of the day whenever I wasn't there."

Nelson: "After loading a skid in the boxcar, another fellow has to truck the skid away and bring in a new skid. We have to wait while the guy does those things, so I smoked a cigarette on the dock—which was permissible. As soon as another skid is brought in I put my cigarette on the load of pallets on the dock because I would still have a few drags left when the next load was finished. The foreman made an issue over it because of the fire hazard. Naturally I knew there was a little hazard, but I told him I had my eyes on it. I still didn't go and put it out just because it might cause a fire.

"I think because I voiced my opinion at the meeting (between Karlson and machinists) Yarby had it in for me."

The other incident took place when Nelson came to work late. Yarby was still taking attendance in the mornings.

Yarby: "I called the roll, and Nelson came in late. I told him to check with the timekeeper. He came after me five minutes later and said, 'Do you expect me to wait around here like this when I could be doing something more valuable back in school?' I told him again that he would have to check with the timekeeper."

Nelson: "I came in late and I said good morning, but he (Yarby) didn't answer. I figured he was busy, so I excused it. I think he definitely had an I'm-too-busy-for-you attitude. He told me, 'You see the timekeeper so he can check you in.' I stood there a few minutes, and the timekeeper didn't come around. I noticed Yarby at the RR dock, and he wasn't busy. I told him I'd like to go back to the school area because I thought it was foolish just to wait and miss school.

"I think he had bad feelings for me because of that break incident. He made such an issue over it at the time.

He just snubbed me. He told me I'd have to wait, and he just walked away."

The following incident took place after the move. The men were taken out of school for half a day. Nelson was asked to clear some scrap cartons and cans from part of the warehouse. The other men were also doing similar work.

Nelson: "I put the scrap on the skid, and asked the forklift driver to move it. He asked me where I should put it. 'Oh, I don't care. Put it by the wall near the desk (Yarby's desk).' I said it innocently, because that's where they put all that stuff. The foreman heard me, and he probably misunderstood what I meant. He probably thought I was just trying to get even by cluttering up the area. This was brought up when Karlson talked to me about my attitude. I didn't defend myself, because I thought I would get myself in more hot water."

Karlson: "The guy showed real impertinence when he said that. When I talked to him, however, I got a feeling of an attitude that was very different than the one he showed while working. Yarby felt I was against him concerning Nelson, and Nelson felt I was against him concerning Yarby."

Even though the machinists were now separated from Yarby and being trained on a full-time basis, on occasion they were called in to work for half a day or so when a real rush job came in. And on these occasions the relationship between them and Yarby was only slightly improved over what it had been. Their work performance continued to be poor, however, and the relationship between the foreman and Nelson was strained, to say the least.

As a result of all this the relationship between the foreman and the superintendent noticeably deteriorated. On the one hand, Yarby thought that Karlson was not backing him up; and on the other, Karlson felt that Yarby was being somewhat petty in his complaints against the machinists and mechanics. They each made the following comments about the situation:

Karlson: "I got the feeling that Yarby didn't think I was backing him up when it came to the situation with the machinists. I feel that, under the circumstances, I did the best I could. That foreman lets little things bother him too much. He should have a better relationship with his men—and with me too. Perhaps he is not the best guy for the job."

Yarby: "I was put in a bad light when Karlson and the personnel supervisor put all the men in school for full days. They didn't even tell me in advance they were going to do that. They stuck up for Nelson and his crew instead of me. What kind of support is that? Now I am even having trouble with my other men. They feel that they also can get away with anything now. What a great place to work!"

Discussion Questions

1. How would you describe the group of machinists in this case? What characteristics of groups do they possess? In what way could these characteristics help or hinder the operations of the company?

2. Do you think that management made any mistakes when they first recalled the machinists and mechanics from field training and assigned them to work in the temporary warehouse? If so, what were they? How could this transition have been handled more smoothly?

3. Why do you think that the behavior of the machinists was different in their school training than it was in their work on the job? What group factors were operating in this situation? How could the management have used the cohesiveness of the group in a more productive manner?

4. Analyze the interrelationships between the following individuals in the case: Yarby, Nelson, and Karlson. What factors led to difficulties in these relationships? How could these relationships be improved?

5. Do you think that Nelson was a good leader? Why, or why not? Do you think he would make a good foreman? Discuss fully.

6. Do you think that the relationship between Yarby and the trainees will ever improve? In what ways would you attempt to improve the situation? How would you go about making any changes?

7. What do you think is going to happen in the future between Yarby and Karlson? Which one is at fault in this situation?

11

the repair ship

Advances in the technological complexity of naval warfare have made it necessary for war ships and auxiliaries to carry large complements of specialists to maintain fighting and servicing ability in addition to the crew required for sea-keeping ability. Unfortunately, the advances in technology have not been accompanied by the requisite advances in administration. As a result, accute conflicts often take place on these ships; and shipboard conflicts, once they occur, can be magnified by the limited environment and rigidity of regulations which exist on a military ship. This case examines such a conflict, which developed between two groups of a small repair ship—the ship's company, and the repair force.

The repair force was responsible for executing the primary mission of the ship—repairs to and logistic support of small combat ships. The personnel of this group consisted entirely of what was formerly referred to in the Navy as "left-arm rates." These men, in the words of Navy Regulations, "were not qualified for command at sea." The rates represented in the group were pipefitters, enginemen, machinists' mates, electricians' mates, damage controlmen, electronics technicians, and storekeepers.

The ship's company was responsible for the operation of the ship. With few exceptions, it was made up of men qualified for command in the event of battle casualties, i.e., boatswains' mates, quartermasters' and gunners' mates, and supported by a small number of radiomen, telemen, yeomen, cooks, and stewards.

The officers of the repair force were all limited-duty officers who had been skilled artisans as enlisted men. The ship's company officers, on the other hand, were all general-line officers who were reservists and had no enlisted experience.

Although it is rarely admitted, there is some stigma attached to "left-arm rates" in the Navy. The term is still quite common even though a change in uniform regulations (stating that all rating badges should be worn on the right sleeve of the enlisted man's uniform) was introduced some ten years ago with the express purpose of avoiding any potential discrimination. On almost any ship in the fleet, there is considerable rivalry between ship's company and the repair crew; but the former consider themselves—and are considered by their below-deck shipmates—to be a higher-status group. Aboard a repair ship, the normal relationship is reversed by the ship's mission. The ship's company functions to transport the repair force to the scene of repair activity.

Shortly after a new commanding officer reported aboard this particular repair ship, the beginnings of a conflict became apparent. The new skipper was extremely proud of his twenty-eight years of service, most of them as quartermaster on sea-going ships. He made it clear to his officers and men that assignment to a repair ship was a degrading experience for him, and immediately set out to regain his self-respect through superior ship handling, ship-keeping, seamanship, and performance in gunnery exercises—all important measures of the ability of a warship captain, but secondary to fulfilling his own role as administrator of repair activity.

In order to ensure achievement of his objective, the captain assumed personal authority for various functions which had been delegated to his officers and petty officers. He supervised loading and unloading of parts and supplies, preservation of topside decks and bulkheads, mooring and unmooring of the ship in the deck department, and acted as gun controller in the gunner department. He also directed scores of other less important activities throughout the ship.

Expressions of resentment appeared almost immediately from subordinates. Requests for transfer increased daily and disciplinary problems became so frequent that an officer was designated permanent trial counsel, so that as many as five special court martials a week could be completed.

The problem below decks was even more serious. Because the captain and his harried line officers and deck-rate petty officers not only ignored the "prima donnas" in the repair force but also treated them with disdain, an ever-widening breach between the two groups developed. Eventually repair officers refused to eat their meals in the ward room with line officers, and this breakdown of social relations quickly spread to the enlisted men's living compartments and mess halls.

The final blow to the repair group came when the commanding officer instructed the officers of the deck that no member of the repair group was to leave the ship on leave or liberty until his seabag was inspected for stolen government property. After this ruling, conditions on the ship began to deteriorate even faster. Because of the absolute authority of the ship's captain, there was little that the repair crew could do through formal channels—especially while at sea. But there were other ways to get back at the captain. The members of the repair crew would obviously malinger on their jobs—and often intentionally do a poor job. Their hope was that the performance of the ship would be rated so poorly that the captain would be dismissed.

Unfortunately this strategy actually backfired, and many members of the repair crew were court martialed for disobeying orders, malingering, deserting, and so on. Ironically, the members of the repair crew finally got what they were after. As a result of all the court martials, the naval command decided to make a formal investigation of conditions on the ship. This investigation revealed the almost total incompetence of the captain, and, as a result, he was "transferred" to a supply depot somewhere in the midwest where he could harmlessly finish out his final years of service before retirement.

No one will ever be able to accurately evaluate the negative effects of the foregoing with regards to the mission of the ship. All I can say is that I would have hated to be on any ship on which "repairs" were done under the conditions described above.

Discussion Questions

1. Who was to blame for the difficulties on this ship? The new captain? The repair crew? The ship's company? The senior command in the Navy? Explain the reasoning behind your answer.

2. What status problems existed between the two basic groups on this ship? How did this affect the operations of the ship?

3. Why did conditions deteriorate so rapidly once the new skipper arrived on board? Would another captain have had any problems? Why, or why not?

4. Assume you were assigned to be the new captain on this ship just after the skipper discussed in this case had been transferred. What conditions do you think you would have found on the ship? What steps would you have undertaken to improve the operations of the ship and the relationships between the repair force and the ship's company? What factors would affect the success of your program? How long do you think your program would take?

12

two troublesome
union–management cases

I am a management consultant whose specialty is union-management relations. I am troubled by two cases on which I am now working, and I want to share with you some of their intricacies.

A. ETHNIC PROBLEMS AT HAMILTON ENGINES

Hamilton Engines is an old company founded nearly a hundred years ago. It has been unionized for the last twenty-five years by an industrial union, and has an outstanding record of labor peace. In fact, there has never been a strike.

In recent years the company has hired more and more Mexican-Americans and has instituted an expensive training program to take anyone with reasonable mechanical potential, even if he doesn't have any facility with English, and develop him into a machinist—or at least someone who can operate the production machines. The supervisors of these men were encouraged to learn Spanish, although very few of them have done so. As a result, many of these employees feel isolated.

The Mexican-Americans also feel somewhat isolated from the union which has been dominated by the other major ethnic group in the plant, the Italians. They control all the top union jobs. However, two of the nine departmental stewards are now Mexican-American. There is an election coming up next month, and there is a Spanish-speaking slate of candidates that will probably give the current leadership a real run for its money because the workforce is now 35% Italian descent, 40% Spanish-speaking, and 25% other.

The Mexican-American group claims that the company and the union have been too cozy for years, and that the union doesn't really represent them. On the other hand, the oldtimers in the plant are worried that their jobs and promotional opportunities might somehow be injured if the plant is dominated by the Mexican-Americans. The company is worried about the conflict because it can't afford to antagonize either group. There are many skilled oldtimers who just are not replaceable.

Hamilton Engines is in a highly competitive industry with relatively low wages compared with other companies in the suburb in which it is located. Therefore it is tempting for a skilled worker, even with seniority, to quit and go elsewhere. Given its particularly low starting wages, Hamilton Engines also depends on the unskilled and untrained Mexican-Americans if it is going to expand in the future. The suburb and surrounding area is becoming largely a white-collar residential area with high rents.

Now here is the specific problem I was called in to deal with:

Two weeks ago, Manuel, the Spanish-speaking candidate for vice-president and chief steward, was accused of having someone else punch his time card so he could leave early. The supervisor of his department said that one of the other workers had even seen Manuel in the parking lot at 2:50 P.M. (The day shift ends at 3:00 P.M.) The supervisor charged him with this, and suspended him for two weeks without pay since this is a serious offense.

Now Manuel has been allowed to return (after three days) and the company has been considering giving him back pay. Manuel said that another worker punched his time card by mistake and didn't tell anyone for fear of being criticized. It is true that he (Manuel) had been out in the parking lot, but only because he suddenly remembered that he might have left his parking lights on that morning since there had been a heavy fog. When he got back he discovered that his time card was already punched out, and he simply left for the day.

The union was now charging that top management had pressured the supervisor into rescinding his disciplinary action to avoid displeasing the Spanish-speaking workers. (The supervisor has told people that top management did get involved in the case.) If it had been any other employee, the union says, the two-week layoff would have stuck; but this was favoritism, and therefore unfair.

Of course Manuel and his friends deny this. They say that the union is out to get him because he is such a strong candidate and has challenged one of the "Old Guard" who is now chief steward. Furthermore, the Mexican-Americans wonder what kind of union is it that wants workers to be penalized. (It should be noted here that the worker who saw Manuel in the parking lot is one of the Italian oldtimers.)

I am not sure how to advise management. Nobody will admit to punching out Manuel's card, and he was seen in the parking lot. The company has always taken a strong stand on this kind of issue, and is proud of its consistent disciplinary policy. The union is threatening to call their first walkout—an all-day "union meeting" to protest favoritism. If they do that, it will really polarize relations between these two ethnic groups. The Mexican-Americans have intimated that if such action is taken, they will move to start their own union.

Discussion Questions

1. In what way did the ethnic differences of the workers complicate the union-management relationship at Hamilton Engines?

2. Do you think the company's attempt to integrate the Mexican-American workers into the social relationships of the organization could have been improved? If so, how?

3. Do you think that management made the right choice in allowing Manuel to come back? Why, or why not?

4. In any case, what can management do now that will ease the situation between the two ethnic groups?

5. What do you see for the future in union-management relations at Hamilton Engines?

6. Are there any general "principles" to follow when you are dealing with an intraunion dispute that also involves the company?

My second case involves a San Francisco publishing company that has never had a union but fears it might be vulnerable now. There have been major cutbacks in this company as a result of declining business, and the employees are worried. Also a number of the younger employees are very active in several liberal or radical (depending on your point of view) organizations in the city that are concerned with racial problems and with changing the government's policies in the international relations field.

Recently this company, Shafer Publishing, has discharged Olivia Adams, one of their women editors. She had been with the company for over five years and had done reasonably well in her job. However, the company says that in recent months she has become more and more hostile on the job. She would insult fellow employees who did not agree with her politics, causing long arguments, and she recently "cursed out" a supervisor who told her that she was wasting too much time.

The final "blow" involved her organization of a meeting concerning women's liberation. She had asked to use the company cafeteria for her group for a meeting the previous week, but had been turned down by the company. Shafer management said that they were deluged with requests for such meetings, and if they acceded to one group they would have to do so for others. Such groups would be likely to leave the area dirty, and this would cause the cafeteria employees to object. More importantly, they didn't think that they should involve the company in community, political, or social issues. These should not be dealt with by their employees and others on company premises or on company time.

Olivia didn't take "no" for an answer, and about three dozen employees came to the cafeteria last Monday. As the company grapevine reports the story, the meeting started with a talk about women's rights, and ended up lambasting Shafer management for failing to promote women to management, discriminating in pay to women, and generally not being an especially estimable company to work for.

The day after the meeting was held, Olivia was fired. Olivia and her friends were incensed and felt convinced that the reason why she was dismissed was because the company disagreed with her on political issues. The company, however, claims that she was discharged because of the deteriorating quality of her work. The company openly admits that she had been a good worker up to the time she became involved in outside political activity, and that because she was so busy with her political work she was now barely able to complete editing one manuscript a month when previously she had easily done four. The dissatisfaction with her performance had been growing over a period of time, and the fact that she was released very soon after the women's liberation meeting was purely coincidental.

Olivia's friends were not at all satisfied with this explanation. Several weeks later the following handbill appeared on nearly every one of Shafer's bulletin boards as well as on bulletin boards in other publishing companies in the city:

WAKE UP BEFORE IT'S TOO LATE

In the last several months eight people have been fired at Shafer's. (Management always say they were laid off for lack of work.)

Will you be next?
Maybe. All the people had been involved in political and/or unionizing activity shortly before they were "let go."
Olivia Adams is an example. In the past five and a half years Olivia had progressed from editorial trainee to area editing supervisor in the Shafer College Department, with steady salary increases. She received her most recent raise on March 2. At 4:30 P.M. on April 23, she was fired without a warning. For the previous two years Olivia had been working with her fellow employees on political issues and was active in Youth Against War and Fascism outside of work. In October 1969, in spite of corporate opposition, Olivia helped mobilize a successful employee walkout in support of the Moratorium. Several weeks later, on her fifth anniversary, two vice-presidents wrote letters praising her for her work and for standing up for her social and political beliefs. In December Olivia helped establish an

employee-sponsored Social Issues Forum to debate such subjects as the war, racism, the Black Panthers, and exploitation of women. At the time of her firing Olivia was participating in the Shafer's Women's Liberation group and had begun handing out union cards.

One afternoon early in April, Olivia and two fellow workers had a discussion about a women's liberation issue. The discussion turned into an argument, which was reported to a department head. Three weeks later, after the upper echelons had engaged in considerable discussion and investigation of the incident and Olivia's behavior in general, they fired her for "obscenity, terrorism, and interfering with the authority of a supervisor," *with the comforting assurance that they would provide her with excellent job recommendations.* The same day a male mailroom employee was also "laid off"; he too had been active in union organizing. Within the next week Olivia's colleagues petitioned for her reinstatement and an explanation of the reasons for her firing. The petition was ignored.

Why was Olivia fired?
Obviously not for poor job performance. And obviously not for saying (. . . . .) (which is what she had said). She was fired because, in trying to organize a union among her fellow workers, she had succeeded, in fact, in threatening those who held power at Shafer—even those who months earlier had praised her. In firing her they hoped to keep other employees from banding together in their common interests.

WE CAN'T LET THEM SUCCEED! Olivia's case is only one of many, but it proves that publishing employees must unite to protect their jobs. We can win job security only by joining together. The FLM is defending Olivia and others who were involved in union activity. Now is the time to begin acting together. DEMONSTRATE June 24, between 12:00 and 2:00 P.M., in front of Shafer's office building to demand Olivia's reinstatement and an end to repression in the publishing industry at large.

Issued by Women in Publishing and Publishing Action Committee.

Discussion Questions

1. *What should management's attitude be toward employee political action at work?*

2. *What happens when community political issues merge with company personnel issues (e.g., women's rights as a general problem, and company promotion policy)? Can they be disentangled?*

3. *Should the company have tried to separate Olivia's work performance from her political activity within the company? How would you suggest that this be done?*

4. *What advice would you give supervisors faced with someone like Olivia, who is a good employee but very politically oriented?*

5. *How do you think the company should respond to the handbill?*

the troubles at wilson

The Wilson Ice Cream Company was organized by Ed Wilson around 1950. Wilson was the proverbial self-made man who had spent most of his adult life starting various business enterprises, mostly restaurants, and building them into profitable going concerns. The ice cream company marked his first attempt at organizing and running a manufacturing concern. The company was started in a very modest fashion. Originally it consisted of a small production department staffed by about three men who made the ice cream, and a retail store housed in the same building in which the product was sold.

After about a year and a half of operating in this manner, Wilson decided to expand his manufacturing facilities and attempt to sell the ice cream wholesale to druggists, restaurants, and supermarkets. In order to accomplish this, he moved the business to a larger plant and hired two salesmen to solicit accounts. Before long, the company had enough accounts to justify the hiring of two full-time route men whose job was to deliver the ice cream from the company's plant to its customers.

Over the next two years the business continued to expand at a fairly rapid rate, considering the competition. By the spring of 1954, the organization consisted of the following:

OFFICE STAFF: six persons including an accountant who doubled as office manager;

SALES DEPARTMENT: five salesmen, each of whom solicited accounts in a designated territory;

A plant manager to supervise the following areas:

SHIPPING DEPARTMENT: two shippers;

REFRIGERATION DEPARTMENT: two refrigeration repairmen;

DELIVERY: five routemen assigned to their own routes;

MISCELLANEOUS PERSONNEL: a carpenter, a sign painter, a janitor, a mechanic, and about ten others in various jobs such as loading trucks, and so on.

One of the primary responsibilities of Harry Fellows, the plant manager, was the supervision of production. While the production foreman took charge of the actual operations, Fellows was responsible for scheduling the items to be produced, purchasing raw materials, and generally ensuring that operations were running smoothly.

The duties which took up the greatest percentage of his time were those concerned with refrigeration maintenance and the installation of new equipment. By this time the company had over one hundred and fifty accounts, and almost all these customers had been loaned at least one ice cream cabinet and compressor unit by Wilson. It was Fellows' responsibility to see to it that these cabinets were repaired as rapidly as possible whenever a breakdown occurred. Not only was this necessary for maintaining good customer relations, but it saved on the amount of spoiled merchandise which the company had to take back as a result of prior agreements with the customers.

Since Fellows had only two refrigerator repairmen, much of his time was spent on the telephone answering the complaints of customers and reassuring them that a repairman would be sent as soon as possible. He also had to arrange for the installation of equipment in new accounts, a job which often took him away from the plant for several hours at a time.

Although a willing and capable worker, these duties took up most of Fellows' day and left him little time to deal with the problems which arose in the shipping and delivery area of the business.

The hardest workers in the company were the routemen. Each of these drivers had a certain number of accounts or "stops" for which he was responsible. His working day didn't end until all his stops had been made. Originally the individual routes were made up by Fellows who worked with Hal Sanders, the head shipper, in accomplishing this task. As the number of customers grew, Fellows was forced to turn his attention elsewhere, and so the duties of assigning new accounts to individual routes was left to Sanders.

The head shipper was not as capable an organizer as Fellows, neither did he possess his facility for coordinating with the salesmen the many details concerned with each new account. As a result, he became little more than a relayer of information between a salesman and the driver in whose area the new account was located.

When a salesman found a prospective customer, he would discuss the prospect with Wilson and together they would work out the details. After receiving Wilson's approval, and subsequently signing up the new account, the salesman would coordinate with Fellows the details of when the necessary cabinet and other equipment could be installed in the customer's store. Next, the salesman would check with Sanders to find out which driver would be servicing the new account. Generally Sanders simply checked the route lists of each driver and provided the salesman with the name of the driver whose existing route was closest to the new account. The salesman would then write a note to the driver and leave it in the shipping office for him to pick up that evening. A typical note of this sort read: "Start deliveries next Monday, Wednesday, and Friday. Be prepared for a big order on Friday as he intends to stock up for the weekend beach crowd." When the driver saw the note that evening he would comment, "That's just impossible. I've already got more stops now than I can handle. Besides, I can't possibly give this new guy a big order on Friday. It's my biggest day, and my truck is already filled to the top. They better get someone else to do it."

These remarks were usually made to Sanders, the head shipper, who would reply that there was nothing he could do about it. The salesman was seldom around at this time, and the drivers had gotten out of the habit of discussing a problem such as this with Fellows.

This method of operations was not limited to notes concerning new accounts. Often the salesmen had special instructions to give the drivers regarding old accounts. These instructions might involve an order to start collecting on delivery from a doubtful account; a change in delivery dates; a reminder for the driver to deliver a signboard to a customer; or one of a dozen other things. More often than not, the same note-writing technique was employed in giving these instructions; and frequently the driver asked a question that Sanders was unable to answer. When the drivers had complaints about excessive demands on the part of the salesmen, or about not being consulted about changes in their routes, and the like, Sanders generally commented to the effect that Wilson let the salesmen run the company and that nobody really cared about the drivers' problems.

The drivers would come in from their routes between 5:00 P.M and 6:00 P.M., and, after handing in their daily receipts, leave for home. However, when two or three drivers finished their routes at the same time, they would hang around the shipping office for ten or fifteen minutes and discuss the day's activities. Since they had no one else to complain to about things that were bothering them, they complained to each other. These discussions became more frequent as weeks went by. Sometimes the first drivers back would wait around for the others to finish their routes, and then they would all leave and have a drink together at a bar down the street.

By this time, the drivers had built up some animosity toward Ed Wilson, the owner of the company. Since heavier routes meant more work for the shippers, these too added fuel to the fire that had been building up throughout the summer. There were few complaints about inadequate pay, but a great many of these concerned the excessive demands being made by the "Old Man" and by the salesmen. Also, some of the new drivers were concerned about the future of their jobs. Since the ice cream business is highly seasonal in the northeast, there was a great deal of speculation about how many men would be laid off when the cold weather set in.

Toward the end of the summer, rumors that the drivers were planning to join a union became more and more frequent. It was well known by all the employees that Wilson was strongly opposed to having a union in his company. This attitude was not at all surprising. He was a strong-willed man who was used to making his own decisions, and no doubt resented the idea of a union taking away any of his prerogatives. In an effort to pacify the drivers, Wilson talked with each man personally.

The drivers, almost to a man, decided that they wanted to be represented by a union—which in this case would be a local of the Brotherhood of Teamsters. Before the formal vote was taken, they set out to enlist the productions workers in their cause. The most outspoken of the production workers who were opposed to unionizing were the three men who had been with the company since it was first organized. They apparently were satisfied with Fellows as a supervisor, and had always been treated fairly. Very likely the younger men in the production department probably had little cause for complaints, but a majority of them apparently gave in to the persuasiveness of the more aggressive truck drivers. In the end, both groups voted for the union.

After the union contract was signed, the drivers, unlike the production workers, quickly adopted the habit of bringing all their grievances—large and petty—to the union's business agent. Even after the signing of the union contract by the truckers and the packers, Wilson made no changes within the organization. He did not seem to think that the joining of the union by these men had anything to do with the conditions in the company.

Over the next couple of years the situation continued to deteriorate—there were a couple of strikes, many more grievances, much shoddy work, high turnover among drivers, and general low morale within the organization. Customer relations were also adversely affected, and the business rapidly started to go downhill. As a result of this, Wilson ended up selling the company at a very depressed price. It seemed unbelievable that a company which had been doing so well could go downhill so fast.

Discussion Questions

1. What was the main difficulty at Wilson?

2. In what ways had Harry Fellows' job changed over the years? How do you think an official "job description" for Harry would have changed over the years?

3. What was Hal Sanders' job? How did he execute it? What problems did this cause? Could management have changed this situation for the better? If so, how?

4. If you were a routeman with this company, how would you view your job? What would be your reactions to the following individuals: Ed Wilson, Harry Fellows, Hal Sanders, and the salesmen?

5. How would you analyze the drivers' animosity toward Ed Wilson? What caused it? How could it have been alleviated?

6. If you had been brought in to advise the new owners of the company, what suggestions would you have made to them in regard to the structure and operations of the company? Discuss fully.

14

two head nurses:
a study in contrast

In external features Floor A and Floor B are very similar. Each has about 30 private and semiprivate beds. On each floor medical patients and surgical patients are cared for by graduate nurses, student nurses, nurses aides, and maids.

FLOOR A

On Floor A, people speak in hushed voices. Conversation is at a minimum. Miss Smith, the head nurse, spends almost all her time at her desk. She gives instructions firmly and unambiguously. The nurses go from room to room caring for patients in a businesslike impersonal manner, and there is little give-and-take between them and the patients.

A. THE HEAD NURSE   Miss Smith's supervisor said of her: "Miss Smith is of the old school. She's really very stern and rigid. She runs an excellent floor from the standpoint of organization and system. It's beautifully organized. She has all her supplies in perfect condition, but she can't handle human relations. Her graduates claim that she treats them like students, watches everything they do, checks up on them all the time, and won't allow them any responsibility. The students claim that Miss Smith gives them only routine, only the small details."

It is generally agreed that Miss Smith is fair and not arbitrary. For example, she makes a conscious effort to

We are indebted to Professor George Strauss for this case.

grant nurses' requests for time off whenever possible, but is strict and uncompromising with nurses who violate regulations. She is uniformly courteous in a formal manner. The following conversation with a member of the dietary department is typical: "I am calling for Miss Wilson, a patient in Room 413, a diabetic case. She would like coffee with every meal. Is that all right? Thank you."

She observes the same rather starchy courtesy whether the pressure of work is relaxed or at its height, and expects the same formal courtesy from her subordinates.

B. THE ASSISTANT   Miss Smith delegates almost no authority to Miss Green, her assistant. When Miss Smith is on the ward, Miss Green shares floor duty with the other nurses and does not work at the desk. When Miss Green is in charge, there is a marked change in the atmosphere. People talk to each other more naturally, and sit around when the work is slack. There is also considerable confusion on the ward.

C. GRADUATE NURSES   The attitude among the younger graduates toward Miss Smith's supervision is expressed in the following quotations:

"Miss Smith runs a very strict floor, and the nurses resent her because she treats them like students."

"When I came here, Miss Smith checked up on everything I did, and that was hard to adjust to. You felt you were a student all over again."

"Miss Smith is off, and the doctors who come here are in a more sociable frame of mind. The whole atmosphere seems to relax. Often we have a nurses' aide mix up a pitcher of lemonade and we have it sitting right down at the desk. If you tried that in the daytime, Miss Smith would have a stroke. When Miss Smith is on, she absolutely does not tolerate any smoking. But when she's off, we all stop and smoke and have coffee."

"I don't pay any attention to Miss Smith any more, and I don't think the other girls do either. You just let what she says go in one ear and out the other. At first it bothered me, and I think it annoyed most of the other girls that she treated us like students. All I say is, 'Yes, Miss Smith,' and go ahead and do what I would have done anyway. We sit around and talk to each other when the work is done, and if Miss Smith asks us to be a little quiet we lower our voices, but we don't attempt to slink around or anything. There was a tendency to do that for a while, but you soon get over that."

The attitude of the older nurses is different as the following quotations show:

"I like working with Miss Smith. I know a lot of the girls complain about her because she's fussy and checks on them. Personally I'd rather work on this floor than anywhere else for exactly that reason. Everything here is done properly. The doctors prefer this floor because this is where the patients get the best care. The other nurses aren't impressed by that. They insist they wouldn't work here because Miss Smith is a fussbudget. They don't seem to care whether the patients get good care or not."

"I picked this floor because I liked the supervision here. I've worked with Miss Smith while I was a student and I knew what to expect. I honestly feel I still need a responsible person nearby to supervise. I need guidance, and therefore I prefer to work on a floor where there is a fairly strict supervisor. On some of the other floors things are too slipshod. Everything is hodgepodge, and it drives me crazy. I like things done in an orderly fashion, and it bothers me very much when everything is slipshod. I don't mean the atmosphere, I mean Miss Smith. She doesn't believe in relaxation at all. As for myself, I prefer to work hard and get it done with and then relax. I can see Miss Smith's point. After all, you have these sick people here and they have to be taken care of. She's got to lay down the law to us to a certain extent. I keep telling my husband how lucky he is to be in his kind of work. Everything in his place is buddy-buddy. But I guess in hospitals it just can't work that way. The head nurse has to be strict in order to get the work done. Isn't that right?"

"Some of the girls are lovely to work with, but others just aren't good at supervising. They don't know how to express themselves. Now when Miss Smith is on, it is altogether different. She knows how to get things done the first time."

D. STUDENT NURSES Miss Smith keeps her students under rigid discipline, and they complain to their supervisor that she gives them only routine work and doesn't allow them to take any responsibility. They feel they learn much less than on other floors. The students ask few questions either of Miss Smith or of the graduate nurses. They rarely talk to anyone.

E. RELATIONSHIPS AMONG WORKERS   All relationships on Floor A tend to be formal and impersonal. There is very little give and take or development of comraderie. Nurses' aides complain that the nurses never teach them anything. Miss Smith divides up the work equably and assigns it clearly, and there is no complaint that some members of the group are slack in carrying out their duties. Yet when Miss Smith is off the floor there is evidence of antagonism among the different workers. The aides say that if they had problems they would take them up with their housekeeping supervisor.

F. PATIENT CARE   The relationship between nurses and patients is rather formal and distant. Patients remain in their rooms, and very few walk about on the floor. Requests by patients and visitors are taken care of promptly and efficiently. The charts are in excellent order, but there is some evidence of slipups in nursing care. In one case, a patient was given the wrong drug and had a severe reaction. During the period when the ward was observed there were three instances of postoperative fever. Once when an intern removed a drainage catheter and forgot to replace it, the error was not corrected for five hours.

FLOOR B

The atmosphere on Floor B is warm and informal. There is a good deal of gossiping and good-natured horseplay, and the girls discuss their problems with one another.

A. THE HEAD NURSE   Miss Rogers, the head nurse, spends only about two-thirds of her time at her desk, and the rest of the time she is on the ward helping with patient-care and chatting informally with workers and patients. She often consults individual nurses, or the entire nursing staff about problems and changes. She expressed her attitude toward supervision as follows:

"The hospital has changed since I graduated. At that time it was just losing the old military discipline and becoming more reasonable in its approach. The present way is much better, on the whole, than the old. I find that if you give people a break, they are more likely to pitch in and help you when you're in a jam. I never could stand this old military discipline stuff."

Miss Rogers is informal in her relationship with her subordinates. Her way of giving an order is typified in this quotation:

"Do you want to go to the pharmacy for me? Gee, that would be swell." Again, when telephoning central supplies, Miss Rogers will say: "Is this you, Betty? Listen, you poor kid, this is me again. I'm sorry, but we've got to have two sets of trays. I thought I'd tell you because if I send the aide down, the poor kid won't get it right."

On the other hand, when the ward is under pressure, Miss Rogers tends to give her answers in an offhand, somewhat distracted way.

B. THE ASSISTANT Miss Rogers deliberately divides authority with her assistant, giving her the jobs of ordering drugs and supplies and superintending the cleaning. She consults her when making decisions. When she is absent, the assistant carries on supervision much as Miss Rogers does. There is little difference in the atmosphere on the ward whether Miss Rogers or her assistant is in charge.

C. GRADUATE NURSES One of the graduate nurses on Miss Roger's floor said: "On this floor anybody can speak up whenever she feels like it, and we get along together fine. The girls on this floor are very good to work with. Miss Rogers is an excellent head nurse, and there is good spirit."

This is rather typical of the attitude of the younger nurses. The older nurses feel somewhat differently:

"Miss Rogers is a very nice person, and all the girls have been lovely to me. But I don't think the organization is as careful as it used to be, and that's why a lot of mistakes are made. It's very easy to forget to give medicine, for instance. It happened to me. Since each nurse is responsible for her own patients, nobody checks up to see whether you've actually given a patient what he's supposed to have. Nobody tells you how you're getting along. I don't know whether I'm doing a good job or not. Maybe I'm forgetting things. Maybe patients complain about me. If so, I never hear of it. I just have to guess that I'm doing all right. I wish that sometimes somebody would come along and check up, and let me know when I do things wrong, and how I can improve myself. I feel that being out so long, I must have plenty of room for improvement."

"Sometimes I work down on Miss Rogers's floor. I was down there last week, and it was exasperating. I had to go down to the drug room myself twice during the morning, and I know that some of the other nurses had to do that too. Well, that's foolish. If the drugs were checked properly in the first place, all the drug orders would have gone down at the same time. That would never happen on Miss Smith's floor because she runs it in a very orderly and systematic way. I don't get any joy out of working on Miss Rogers's floor because things are done just too sloppily."

D. Student Nurses Miss Rogers said that she enjoys teaching, but has some problems in maintaining discipline. Students seem to be accepted as an integral part of the social group. They take part in informal discussions and are free to ask any questions they wish.

E. Relationships Among Workers The relationship among the different groups of workers on Miss Rogers's floor is easy and informal. Some of the nurses' aides address Miss Rogers by her first name, and she calls them by nicknames. There is a strong spirit of comraderie throughout the ward. On the other hand, Miss Rogers does not assign tasks to each worker in a clearcut specific way, and consequently there is some tendency to shirk certain tasks. As one nurses' aide put it:

"They just expect all of us to get the work done. If one person lies down on the job, it would mean that the other person does that much more. Evidently they don't stop to think who does what. We've got a little bit of jealousy. A good boss could straighten it out."

The nurses' aides on Miss Rogers's floor say that if they had a problem they would first take it up with her.

F. Patient Care The relationship between patients and workers on the ward is easy and informal. The patients are part of the social group. They wander in and out of their rooms. At times they join in the chatting of a group of nurses, and even run small errands for the nurses. The nurses call them by their first names.

When the work is heavy, however, Miss Rogers and the nurses tend to be brusque with the patients. They do not always meet the patients' requests or those of their visitors promptly. Charts are not maintained with scrupulous care.

Although some of the older nurses feel that the loose supervision is likely to result in slipups in nursing care, none were noted during the period of observation.

Patients who once have been on Floor B not infrequently ask that they be sent there again at the time of a second admission. Some doctors also request that their patients be admitted to this floor because of the good psychological care which they receive.

Discussion Questions

1. Is it possible to say that either of these floors was "better" than the other in an overall way? Why, or why not?

2. Would it be possible to supervise a floor so as to combine the good features of both A and B floors, and minimize the less desirable features of each? Discuss fully.

3. What kind of patients would receive better care on Floor A, what kind on Floor B?

4. Why was there such a marked difference in attitude on the part of younger and older nurses toward the two supervisors?

15

ron, the steel man

This is a report of my observations at the D. H. Lowry Company, a small manufacturing plant on the outskirts of Fairfield, New Jersey. I worked in this plant for ten months, from November 1961 to September 1962. During that time I shared a twelve-foot square glass-enclosed office, located in a corner of the factory, with plant superintendent Ron Mancini. My job was to do plant clerical work for three hours every morning.

The Lowry Company fabricates steel and aluminum windows for commercial and industrial buildings. A Dun and Bradstreet report, completed in January 1962, indicated that the company had suffered a sharp decline in sales and earnings following a strike of several months' duration in 1959; also large losses on window installation contracts, an activity which has since been dropped. Because of the drop in sales and cutback in production, the home office and principal plant was moved from Manhattan to Fairfield two years ago. Along with this move, a large reduction in personnel took place.

Over the past several years, as aluminum windows became competitive with the more traditional steel windows, there has been severe price competition in the metal window industry. Although aluminum is more expensive than steel, the cost of its fabrication is far lower because equipment and labor per unit costs are lower. Forecasts for industrial and commercial construction in 1962 were for a small increase during the year.

OPERATIONS

The operation sequence in the window business is as follows:

An inquiry is made by the general contractor, a quotation is made by the prospective supplier, and, if satisfactory, an order is placed by the contractor. Sales and engineering handle the process until final approved drawings are received from the architect. At this point, the inquiry becomes an order and working drawings are prepared by engineering and sent to the plant for fabrication. Installation is done by special subcontractors.

Orders customarily specified shipping dates as "the week of . . . ." Official company policy called for six weeks manufacturing lead time based on allowances of one week for engineering to prepare final working drawings, four weeks for fabrication, and one week for leeway. Any steel window made by the company could be fabricated in four working days. An aluminum window took two and a half days. The plant superintendent handled all fabrication scheduling.

Steel windows are made in three operations—cutting, sash assembly, and window framing. Steel-working equipment for the gauges used in windows is large and expensive compared with equipment used for aluminum or wood (much of which is interchangeable).

Aluminum windows are far more simple to fabricate. They can be detailed on one drawing and require less equipment, less space, and less time to make.

The Lowry factory was a one-story L-shaped building, twenty feet behind a haphazardly remodeled house containing executive and clerical offices. The plant superintendent's office was located at the factory entrance in a small glassed and heated area. It overlooked the approach from the office on one side, and the main factory floor on the other.

This floor had aluminum cutting and assembling operations on the far side adjacent to the short leg of the L, which was empty except for one designer's office. Steel cutting operations were done directly in front of the superintendent's office. Steel sash assembling and window framing were carried on in an adjacent area not visible from the office. At the extreme other end of the building there was a second-floor loft where the draftsmen worked.

The production manager supervised quotations (one man); engineering (a chief and six draftsmen); and plant operations. The plant superintendent had a foreman in charge of steel windows with three lead men under him.

Also there was a lead man for aluminum windows; he had one assistant.

The plant usually employed about 65 production workers. This was reduced to 40 odd at the bottom of the slow season (midwinter) and rose to 75 in the summer rush season when most of the experienced men put in overtime.

RON, THE PLANT SUPERINTENDENT

Ron Mancini was plant superintendent at Lowry. A cocky little man in his late thirties, he had worked for the company for sixteen years and had built, installed, and repaired steel windows. He really liked steel windows. He hated paperwork. And he thought that aluminum windows were "really junk, baby. Any jerk can knock them off with a handsaw in his own garage. There's nothin' to it, and that's all them cheap things are—nothin'!"

Ron had started at Lowry as a machinist. He was a union enthusiast, but he told me that "when ya get to be a foremen, there's some things ya just gotta give up. It ain't all gravy, believe me. But a buck's a buck, and you gotta think of your future."

Mr. Samuels, the seventy-year-old chairman of the board, was the only executive in the company for whom Ron ever expressed complete admiration. "He really knows windows. He even knows them better than I do. And believe me, there ain't many guys in the world you can say that about. And none around here except him. You can't fool him on a thing. I wouldn't try, and he knows it. He's a real gentleman, too, but he always talks to me sort of like I was his son or something. I'd do anything Mr. Samuels told me to. And he gave me all this when we moved out here." (He meant the plant and being superintendent of it.)

Phil D'Arrigo, the thirty-year-old steel window foreman, was Ron's closest working associate and the only other employee about whom Ron never made critical comments. "He's a good man. You can trust him, and he never acts wise."

Mr. Felton had joined Lowry shortly after the move to Fairfield, and had been given the title of production manager a few months before I arrived.

"I don't know why they ever did that," Ron said. "Felton used to be some sort of an accountant or something.

Production. Hah! He don't know nothin' about production. He's just a pencil-pusher. He thinks you make windows by writing a lot of memos and making up new forms for people to fill out. He's always coming around with a fistful of papers and bothering me. You should hear the dumb questions he asks."

Ron spent his time bounding back and forth between the factory floor and his office. He showed the welder how to make them hold on that new job; he found a tool-and-die man who didn't drink; he explained to me how to order hardware and handle bills of lading; he checked to see if the truck had arrived to pick up that rush job.

He avoided talking to some expediters on the phone, and he tried to reach others. He tried to keep his immediate boss from finding out how late some jobs were running, and made good on a promise to the sales manager to get out a new job in two weeks.

He listened to the state employment man who tried to convince him to hire paroled prisoners, and he helped carry a seriously bleeding workman to the hospital because the ambulance would take longer. He threatened a franchiser with removal of the vending machine when the men, who didn't lie, kicked about losing quarters.

He cracked jokes with the Underwriters Laboratory inspector, blasted the engineering chief for an incredible mistake, then "put out the fire" with a two-minute phone call. He fought with installers who said that his windows were out of square; phoned his wife once a day to tell her that things were fine at the plant; and he told a bright young kid he might get to be pretty good at the window business some day "if he stuck around and kept his nose clean." He also checked the drawings on every job that came into the shop; and he checked the diets of the maintenance man's twin grandsons.

And the plant shipped three thousand windows while I was there.

Ron consistently treated the coffee break like a ceremonial rite. The men had ten minutes between bells, and he would watch to see when they were almost all back in the plant and then tell Phil or me to go get coffee and cake. We three would sit in the office. Phil did not have a desk, and used a work table in the assembly shop—but he always came into the office for coffee. Ron used the time for telling jokes and stories.

About once a week or so, though never on a regular

basis, Jerry Robins, the aluminum lead man, and his assistant, Cal would come into the office at coffee time. They never came in unless Ron waved to them through the window, and I never noticed them waiting to be asked. When the four men were together they usually talked among themselves about funny things that had happened in the plant recently or about "the old days."

Ron added to the conversation, but did not "hold court" as he did when only Phil and I were there. Cal had a hard time describing any situation without using a lot of four-letter words, but he struggled to think of substitutes because I was present. Once they all came in together with a general air of anticipation and wearing broad smiles. Ron said, "G'wan over an' lick some postage stamps or something, baby, I gotta hear this story an' I gotta hear it right."

Jerry and Cal always left the office immediately when the work bell rang. Phil left a minute or two later. Ron always continued to engage me in small talk for at least another five minutes, and usually told me to ignore the telephone if it rang during this time.

I saw Mr. Samuels and Ron interact only once (it was on this occasion that Ron expressed his sentiments toward the man). Mr. Samuels came to the plant office with working drawings of a sample steel window that he wanted made and shipped immediately. The older man had a courtly manner, and was quiet and concise in his directions. He ended by saying, "I have promised it will be shipped by Friday." It was. And Ron never referred to it to others in the organization, who were putting considerable pressure on him at that time because of delay deliveries on prior orders.

MR. FELTON'S EFFECT ON RON

Mr. Felton thought that the solution to the problem of late deliveries lay in a successful search for the one guilty person who had "caused" the delay. "Are you responsible for this?" was his frequent, angry demand. "I intend to get to the bottom of this," was another favorite opening gambit.

Felton's attempts to solve problems revolved around the formation of new rules, which he set forth in memos and circulated to all department heads. In fact, these were usually naively stated copybook "principles" which Felton did not have the knowledge to make operational, and which Ron, therefore, ignored.

Felton's directives, however, did have the effect of creating some temporary alliances between Ron and drafting chief Fred, when the drawings had run behind schedule, and between Ron and the sales manager when customers complained. Occasionally the men managed to work off a good deal of tension by discussing their common enemy —Mr. Felton. These short informal talks were also useful to the participants in giving each other a clearer insight into their own problems via "what Felton doesn't realize about my problems is . . ." explanations.

One type of steel window as well as all the aluminum ones required factory installation of spring balances (a patented device that permits a window to balance at any selected level for ventilation) which were shipped by truck from the Lowry plant in Racine, Wisconsin. Although balances are all of the same basic design, they vary with the weight of the sash to be carried. Balances were ordered by engineering and recorded on receipt by me. Four weeks lead time was customary.

One day Ron discovered that none of the balances for a large job, which was nearing completion, had arrived. In fact, they had not even been ordered. There had already been considerable difficulty and delay with this order, and the sales manager and Mr. Felton had complained bitterly to Ron about it. He was appalled when he found out about the balances. "Wally (the Racine plant manager) will just have to ship them day after tomorrow," he said.

I expressed amazement that this could be done. Ron said, "It'll throw him in a real bad hole, and I know it. I hate to do it to him, but I gotta. And he knows I wouldn't kid him. Listen, Wally and I understand each other. Every once in a while he slips a little junk in here on a big order where he knows it won't throw me in a hole, and I go out and adjust them balances myself—and nobody's the wiser. He don't do it too often, only when he has to. It's a tough life trying to run a plant. He and I play it straight with each other."

Ron telephoned Wally. The balances were shipped two days later.

In the late spring a memo arrived signed by the president and Mr. Felton, directing that there be no more overtime because of the company's difficulty in obtaining material at reasonable costs. When I expressed some surprise, because recently orders had markedly increased and I wondered how we'd meet deliveries, Ron said, "The union contract is coming up for talks next month, and the company wants to play poor. It won't make any difference, but it's the way you gotta play the game."

Ron attended several meetings on the union contract. He never discussed any of the details, but he did remark, "That Felton shows himself for a fathead, and Mr. Samuels knows it. He oughta have the sense to stay out of what he don't understand."

A NEW MAN ARRIVES—BURT

In late February, five very large aluminum jobs for New York public schools came through as "will advise delivery" orders. ("They're gonna be a mess," was Ron's comment.) During the next month, aluminum orders continued to arrive in far greater quantity than ever before; and steel orders fell.

Ron spent more and more time with Jerry trying to keep the windows coming. He hired new men, used more overtime, but the work still piled up and deliveries fell further behind. I spent more and more time on the telephone trying to fend off irate contractors. Mr. Felton constantly charged over to the office. Cal hurt his hand and was out for a week. The treasurer, the sales manager, the drafting chief, and even the cost accountant started coming to the office to try to talk to Ron. But he was always out on the floor, and never called them back when he did come in to sit down for a few minutes.

Then suddenly the pressure was off. The phone ceased ringing every minute, the office men stopped coming, an eerie sort of normal descended, and some of the most pressing orders even got shipped.

Two weeks later Burt came to work for Lowry. He was in his early thirties, a quiet sort of chap with an earnest manner; he was a college graduate, and had worked in an aluminum window plant for five years. He said he was working for Mr. Felton, helping out on aluminum.

During the first week he came to the office only three or four times, usually looking for one of the other managers. But he never wandered through the plant or talked to any of the men. The first direct request I heard him make of Ron was, "Is there anything in the files on those

five school jobs which I could look at for a couple of days?"
(There were only bare order sheets, and Ron gave them
to him.) The next week Burt asked short questions about
scheduling and materials on a few other big aluminum
jobs. He never made any disparaging comments, and he
never carried any papers down with him.

A few days later Ron asked Burt a question about a
steel job. Burt replied, "Gee, Ron, I just don't know
much about steel. All my experience has been in aluminum, and that's not a lot of help. I'll try to figure out
something if you want me to." But Ron thanked him and
turned down the offer.

The next day Ron asked Burt a question about an
aluminum job. Burt answered it very simply along the
lines of "we had a problem like that once before and we
solved it this way." Ron asked him if he would come out
on the floor and look at the job. When Ron came back he
said, "That Burt, he's a pretty good guy!"

Within a week Ron was initiating questions on aluminum to Burt. Within two weeks Burt had put a desk in
the unused L next to the aluminum jobs. He set up a
new layout for the section, installed new equipment, and
got the jobs out. Felton never appeared in the office any
more; the steel jobs moved more smoothly, and the pressure was off Ron.

Two months later Ron told me that all the files were
to be moved that night to Burt's area, and that I would
work there from then on. It appeared that Burt was a
man on the way up in the organization.

Discussion Questions

*1. What effect does a period of hard times, such as
experienced by D. H. Lowry Company, have on the company's management policies? Do they turn more aggressive? Cautious? Or what? What about the effect on personnel policies?*

*2. In carrying out the duties of his job, Ron was in-
volved in a multitude of activities. How important do
you think these were to the success of the company?*

*3. Analyze Ron's interactions with the following: (a)
the case writer (who was a woman), (b) Mr. Samuels,
(c) Mr. D'Arrigo, (d) Mr. Felton, (e) Jerry and Cal, (f)
Wally, the Racine manager, and (g) Burt. How were these
interactions instrumental in the supervision of the plant?*

4. How would you evaluate the managerial abilities of (a) Ron, (b) Mr. Felton, (c) Mr. Samuels, and (d) Burt? Which one of these men would you most have liked to work for? Why?

5. Why do you think Ron responded to Burt in the way he did? Given the fact that the case writer only worked during the morning hours, do you think something might have happened that she didn't know about concerning this situation?

6. What do you think lies in the future for steel man Ron, and aluminum man Burt? If Burt is on the way up, does this mean that Ron is on the way down? If so, is this good or bad for the company? Why?

7. What do you think the relationship between Ron and Burt might be like in the future?

16

terry,
the disappearing supervisor

Faultless Engineering, Inc., was a medium-sized consulting engineering firm; its specialty was design and plant layout work, but occasionally specialized textile and paper machinery design jobs were accepted, more as a service to the larger clients than as a source of revenue to the company. To provide this service, a thirty-man force was maintained on a full-time basis.

When a new job was accepted, one of the partners of the firm would appoint an older machine designer to head the project, and the chief designer would then select any men from the thirty-man pool who were not currently assigned to another project. Although this lack of formal organization occasionally created personnel problems, the jobs came at such infrequent intervals, and were so varied in size and scope, that this arrangement was a necessary evil for the company.

Most of the members of the machine design pool had only worked for Faultless Engineering for about five years, but they all had had more than eight years of experience in this business. Because of the specialized nature of their work, none of the pool members (with the exception of the chief designers) ever associated with individuals outside of the group. Within the group, however, every man was well known to his fellow members even though they were geographically separated within the company's office areas, and they frequently consulted each other on various problems which arose during the course of their design projects. For the most part, the amount of respect that each member of the group commanded from his fellow workers was directly proportional to the length of time he had been engaged in machine design work; length of service within the company had little or no bearing on an individual's prestige.

Once a machine design "section" was formed to handle a specific job for a client, the chief designer performed the necessary coordination functions with the chief engineer of the project. The chief engineer was usually concerned with the project's plant layout and building design; thus, the machine design section assigned to the project acted as an autonomous unit. The chief designer was responsible only to the chief project engineer, who managed his design crew as he saw fit.

It was during the company's busiest season that a problem emerged. Mr. Vinson, one of the senior engineers of the company, was assigned as project engineer for three new jobs within a two-week period. Since all three jobs involved machine design, and since he knew nothing about the subject, he appointed three designers—Terry, Brian, and Joel—to head the machine design phase for each of the three projects. Terry was the oldest of the three designers and had more than thirty-five years experience in the business. Unfortunately, he had had a nervous breakdown six years earlier and his health at this time was not of the best. Brian and Joel each had fifteen years experience, and both men were easygoing individuals.

In the beginning, Mr. Vinson spent most of his time talking to Terry about the various details that his section would be expected to solve; he also asked him for much information concerning machine design in general. Mr. Vinson often talked to Terry's men about matters concerning the machine design phase of the project, and Terry would hear of these conversations some time after Mr. Vinson returned to his own office. Terry never complained to Mr. Vinson about interrupting the design section; but from the time that these "private conversations" began, Terry told each of his men only as much as was absolutely necessary for each of them to do his work.

Within two weeks, Terry saw Mr. Vinson only when he needed drafting supplies for his section or when he submitted the section's weekly progress report. Also, he gave every member of his section explicit instructions to tell Mr. Vinson to consult only with him when Vinson came around for information. Although each member of this group had the highest regard for Terry, they did not wish to antagonize Mr. Vinson and continued to answer Mr. Vinson's questions if and when he asked for information.

About one month after the job began, Mr. Vinson suddenly stopped his daily visits to Terry's section. He now spent his time with the leaders of the other two design groups. At first Terry seemed happy with the situation, but Mr. Vinson also stopped consulting Terry about machine design matters. Neither did the other chief designers come over to see Terry, and he told his section members that his group was getting the "silent treatment" and that the section would have to carry on alone.

About this time Terry began to take time off from work. At first it was just a day or two every other week; but within two months, Terry was absent for periods of a week or ten days every month. Members of the machine design section were becoming uneasy because they frequently completed the designing Terry had assigned to them while he was absent, and then they had to appear busy until he returned. It wasn't found out until later that at this time Terry was actively looking for a job elsewhere. As a result, Terry had designed the current project in such a way that, when he left, the muddled condition of the job would make the rest of the group look bad in the eyes of the company's central management. The design members of Terry's section did not know where he had been or what he had been doing during his periods of absence from the job.

Terry had been away from his work for more than two weeks when one of the older members of the group notified Mr. Vinson about the conditions that existed in Terry's section. Mr. Vinson immediately transferred Randy, a young graduate engineer, into Terry's section and put him in charge until Terry returned. When Mr. Vinson introduced Randy to the members of the section, he was called away on another matter before he had a chance to tell Randy the nature of the project. Randy spent the next week talking with various members of the section and familiarizing himself with the different features of the job. During that time, Randy tried to approach Mr. Vinson with problems and questions; but Mr. Vinson was either too busy to talk with him, or else he did not know the answers.

One week after Randy arrived, Terry returned to work.

He was approached by Randy to answer questions which Mr. Vinson had left unresolved. Terry was in a position to outline the entire project to the young engineer, but he did not choose to do so. Instead he privately insinuated to the rest of the group that Randy was Mr. Vinson's "inside man" and should not be trusted. As a result of these conversations, nobody within the section knew just who was in charge. And Mr. Vinson had not informed Randy or Terry as to who should be the leader.

The efficiency and output of this section fell even lower than it had been previously. Randy and Terry were not speaking to each other; intrigues and rumors were rampant; and members of other sections began to refer to Terry's section as "the orphans" and "the awkward squad." One by one, members of this section started looking for new jobs outside the company. Those who remained faithful to the firm began to petition for transfer to Brian and Joel's sections.

Discussion Questions

1. Would you make any suggestions as to another way that Faultless Engineering might handle these specialized design jobs? Do you think that Faultless should be doing these jobs at all? Why, or why not? Discuss some of the problems in doing "service" jobs.

2. How would you describe the interpersonal dynamics of the machine design pool? What type of group is this? Discuss the various types of groups which an organization is likely to have.

3. What would you say about the prestige of the machine design group? What factors lend prestige and status to a group in an organization?

4. Discuss the division of authority and responsibility between the chief engineer and the chief designer for each special project. Do you think that this is the best type of relationship? Discuss. How would you organize such activities?

5. Assess the managerial capabilities of Mr. Vinson. What do you think caused him to behave as he did? If you were Mr. Vinson's immediate supervisor, what directives would you give him?

6. Why do you think that Mr. Vinson suddenly stopped attending to Terry's section? Would you agree with Terry's assertion that his group was being given the "silent treatment"? If so, why? If you had been Terry, would you have handled the situation with Mr. Vinson differently? If so, how?

7. Assume that you were one of the designers in Terry's section. How would you have reacted to his absence? Would you have gone earlier to management? What would you have said? What effect did the closeness of the group have on the total situation with Terry?

8. What type of training did Mr. Vinson give Randy? If you had been Mr. Vinson, what would you have done instead?

9. Discuss Mr. Vinson's reaction when Terry finally returned to the job. How did this affect the situation?

10. Assume that you were Randy. How would you feel about this whole situation? What do you think you could do to alleviate it, if anything?

11. What do you think is going to happen in the future with Terry's section? What ramifications could this have for the company? What do you think can be done?

12. Analyze the deficiencies of management at Faultless Engineering.

17

chuck, the manager

At age fifty-two, Chuck Fielding had spent many years as a successful engineer in various companies. He was well known in the fields of mechanical and aeronautical engineering. Chuck, however, wanted to get more involved in management. Therefore, when one of his old friends at Propwash, Inc., offered him a job as the head of the Production Engineering Department at their Thrust Division, Chuck enthusiastically accepted. Propwash, Inc., was a major aerospace firm. Chuck knew that if he did a good job in their Thrust Division, his future would be most promising.

The first thing Chuck realized was that the Thrust Division was far different from the rest of Propwash. Thrust was strictly in the business of developing and producing missiles and space vehicles. In 1956, Thrust had won the contract for a high performance ballistic missile. Numerous other contracts for additional space vehicles and missiles had been forthcoming, and Thrust Division had now grown to the point where sales were as large as the rest of Propwash combined.

The division was organized on a Project basis normally in line with the governmental agency (Army, Navy, NASA, and so forth) supporting the Project. Thrust's general organization chart appears below.

Primarily the projects were concerned with the design, development, testing, and production of a particular product. They also were concerned with improving the existing product and producing any logical follow-ons. The Central and Research organizations were concerned with the design, development, testing, and production, which was common to all or most projects, or alterna-

95

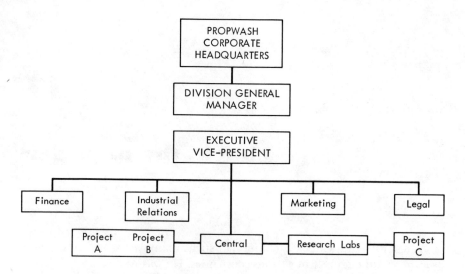

FIGURE 1

organization chart for Propwash, Inc.

tively with projects not yet sufficiently developed to be products. The Production Engineering Department was in Central.

PRODUCTION ENGINEERING

Fielding was amazed by what confronted him. The organization was in complete disunity. The engineers weren't engineering, and the department was the least popular in the company. A combination of events had led to this situation.

First, there was underutilization of manpower. Some of the men had no jobs to do. They were coming in and filling a desk, or inventorying labs, or just sitting about chatting. One of the most popular statements among the few younger engineers who had not as yet left was, "Where else can I be semiretired at the age of twenty-five?" Second, the men showed complete disgust with their technical leadership. Many of the men felt that the company "would buy a project for making gold out of cowdung if you talked fast enough."

Besides this, it appeared that this department was regarded as a joke by the majority of the other departments in the organization. Chuck quickly realized that many sections of the Thrust Division would not give his department any work at all. Soon after he accepted the job another project manager at his level said, "I'm sorry, Chuck. I can't give you any work. It's not your fault, I know, but I just can't trust the level of work I get from those people who work for you. Why, a year and a half ago one of them sent me a report, and I know some of the data he gave me was phony. Since then, when I've needed development work, I've gone to outside engineering companies."

Others told him that although the work was adequate, the time getting this work done was just too long to permit relying on Production Engineering.

Three years before Chuck took over, Grant Adams had been made manager of the Production Engineering group. He had received a Ph.D. from the University of California in Chemical Physics at the age of twenty-three, and had worked for NASA in the Langley Research Center for about ten years prior to coming to work for Propwash. During this period he had written voluminous research monographs, and had become an outstanding voice in the early development on stress corrosion and fatigue in high-strength stainless steel alloys. In hiring Adams, Propwash followed a continuing policy of bringing outstanding minds into the corporation. Such minds presented the basis on which Propwash had built its eminence in the industry, and such names as Adams also helped when they appeared on proposals.

Adams, however, had a tremendous weakness for performing detailed studies. He would often accept jobs for the department, and become involved in the specific details of the study rather than in effecting a solution to the entire problem. Because of the tremendous rush to meet schedules in Project, the department frequently was late in issuing reports. The production groups found that they couldn't wait for reports, and therefore either did the work themselves or sent it all the way back down the work flow to Research.

Adams found that he was losing work. As he lost work, the supervisors of the groups under him became frustrated and angry. Soon they began going out to drum up business on their own, relying upon their own reputations within Propwash. However, the type of work each supervisor obtained varied considerably. Hence some got jobs which involved fairly basic research. On the other extreme, others were troubleshooting in the shops.

Eventually management became aware that Production Engineering was a bottleneck, that no work of significance was being accomplished, and Adams was transferred into Research in a staff capacity with a small lab and four assistants.

Adams was followed by a succession of three acting managers. Each lasted from two to three months. During this phase, the number of engineers fell from 100 to about 60. About 20 men resigned. The majority of the remainder either voluntarily transferred to other departments, or were asked to transfer. During this period the Production Engineering Department sank to its low point. The few budgeted man-hours for remaining research went to one or two of the faster-talking engineers who could convince the nontechnical acting managers that they had a good idea. On the other hand, most of the others were running about troubleshooting in the shops.

This was the situation when Chuck Fielding became manager.

FIELDING'S FIRST STEPS

His first step was to decide on the role of his department. He quickly learned that in the Thrust Division, Research was responsible for developing the fundamental concepts which eventually evolved into products. At some time his department would be consulted for input regarding materials, processes, and fabrication techniques. Ultimately the result of these efforts, both separate and joint, would be engineering reports. These would then be forwarded to the project or the central development group to build a prototype.

Although there might come a time when the implementation of the engineering report required that Fielding's department be consulted, he decided that troubleshooting in the shop was *not* desirable in that the individual projects had liaison engineers who were specifically responsible for eliminating causes of trouble in their project. But these liaison engineers resented the fact that the Production Engineering people were directly contacting the shops for such work. Invariably, if Production Engineering solved a problem, they claimed the credit. On the other hand, problems and failures were credited to the liaison engineers.

Chuck also found that pure research was outside of the jurisdiction of his department. First, it didn't have the personnel or equipment resources. Second, the people "up on the hill in Research" jealously guarded their realm in the company.

The role of his department was from applied research through development. He could characterize the flow of a project as:

pure research	applied research and development	prototype	product

Fielding's department interfaced with the several research groups on one side, and with the manufacturing engineers on the other. In the case of searching out trouble spots, he found it desirable to receive input from the liaison engineers and deal with their problems in a *consultative* manner, with the ultimate decision as the responsibility of the project liaison engineer.

DEALING WITH THE SUPERVISORS

As noted above, each supervisor in the Production Engineering Department was out drumming up business on his own. This resulted in tremendous instability in the relationship with the interfacing departments. Before Chuck had an opportunity to act on this problem, a situation arose that precipitated a change.

Ned Thomas was the supervisor of the metallurgy group. He was loud and vociferous, and always ready to get into a fight. Three months after he arrived, Chuck received an angry phone call from a project manager a full level above him who stated that Ned had been in his office that afternoon and attempted to negotiate a job with him. When he refused, Ned slammed a fist on his desk and called him an "s.o.b."

When Ned came back, Chuck called him into his office and asked why Ned had taken it upon himself to interact with someone at that level. Ned told Chuck to "mind his own damn business," and that he didn't intend to let "any damn manager mess up jobs I've spent weeks getting." Ned shouted rather loudly, and most of the people in the area heard him. After Ned stormed out, Chuck made arrangements to have him transferred out of his department.

From his previous jobs Chuck had become friendly with Mel Franks, a division manager at Propwash. Mel had been a driving, energetic technical manager. Two years ago, however, Mel had had a heart attack. After ten months of illness, he returned to a technical staff position. He was eager to perform in the Propwash environment, but his days of fighting the wars on the ladder of line management were over.

Mel was well liked, and knew almost everyone. He had many contacts, and some of these contacts were at a high level. He was easygoing, and willing to deal with people in a far more passive manner than the younger and more aggressive supervisors. Chuck made him his staff assistant, ostensibly as an administrator and personnel man.

Chuck then called in the supervisors and made it clear that new business would be cleared on the department level. It was all right for supervisors to meet with other supervisors in order to carry on new business or to discuss the old. It was not all right to go out to drum up new business. Mel had that job, and he would commit the department to new jobs.

DEALING WITH THE ENGINEERS

Mel moved adroitly in gathering new jobs. As this phase progressed, new assignments began to arrive. Chuck attempted to divide the labor so that junior engineers got assignments that would involve following a job from the early stages to the final report. Senior engineers either performed consultative work, or led a group of junior engineers. In this way, the young engineers were able to function in their field, gain useful experience, and were kept busy. On the other hand, senior engineers were able to use their experience and gain new experience leading the younger men.

Chuck also added a technical staff man to his personal staff. Recruited from another department at Propwash, Marty Hanson was a capable and intelligent senior staff engineer. He was able to provide Chuck with a strong measure of technical support in evaluating the work of the department.

The engineers were beginning to get work, and apparently felt that the work was meaningful. To further help this situation, Chuck attempted to reach an understanding with Research as to the approximate lines of jurisdiction. Then he embarked on a program of obtaining contracts from outside agencies, such as NASA, for projects within his agreed-on jurisdiction, and reached an understanding with Research on mutual support arrangement for such projects. By assigning engineers to outside assignments, he gave his men the opportunity to broaden their experience with outside contractors. In addition they had the opportunity to travel, which was a desirable fringe benefit for the men. At the same time Chuck began to encourage his people to attend more professional societies' meetings and to study toward advanced degrees.

CONCLUSION

As time went on, the Production Engineering Department greatly improved its operations. Chuck found that his control of the department was possible without crossing the natural jurisdictional lines which separated his department from interfacing departments. In turn, he found that these interfacing departments were more willing to deal with him on an equitable basis.

Mel was more capable than he could have expected in carrying on the day-to-day external relationships which were always necessary. Moreover, the supervisors grew to respect Mel's ability in these situations and looked to him for aid.

The supervisors quickly learned that Chuck meant business. They discovered that so long as they carried on their interactions with external departments and with the engineers within the parameters which Chuck had established, they would be permitted a great degree of autonomy in their relationships.

As productivity and morale of the PE department improved, Chuck Fielding's reputation grew. Early this year Chuck moved up to one level below the director of Central. The general feeling was that he would continue to move up.

Discussion Questions

1. *What major problems confronted Chuck when he began his job in the Production Engineering Department of the Thrust Division? Were these problems in any way*

predictable, given the industry and the growth at Thrust? If so, how?

2. What do you think caused the problems Chuck encountered in the Production Engineering Department? Explain your reasoning.

3. Do you think Thrust used Grant Adams' skills intelligently? What would you have suggested?

4. Analyze each step Chuck took in upgrading the operations of the Production Engineering Department. How effective were these steps? Carefully analyze the change in interrelationships, caused by Chuck's actions, between the various departments in the organization.

5. Do you think that the engineers in the Production Engineering Department were more company oriented or profession oriented, i.e., locals or cosmopolitans? Discuss fully.

6. Chuck's program appeared to be a success. Why do you think this was so? Examine all factors.

7. Do you think Chuck will continue to move up at Thrust? Why? Does Chuck's success with the Production Engineering Department ensure his success in a higher position? Why, or why not? How would you assess Chuck's chances for success in a higher position?

18

summer camp

During the summer of 1969, I spent six weeks at an Army Reserve Officers' Training Corps camp.

The physical organization of the camp conformed to what everyone has either experienced or heard concerning "army living." In the type of personnel involved, however, the camp differed from the typical. The cadre were Regular Army officers and NCO types drawn from ROTC detachments at colleges and universities across the United States. We (the trainees) were all college students who had just completed the junior year at our undergraduate institutions. We all had been exposed to Army-oriented training for the past three years, but only to the extent it had been incorporated into the academic environment.

For the majority of us (the exceptions being students from the more military-oriented schools such as VMI, who had lived a military life rather than just a scholastic one) enrollment in the ROTC program consisted in the main of classroom work in the fields of military operations and "drill" periods which gave us a very basic feel for military leadership in practice. Generally we were (with the exceptions noted above) about equal in our exposure to military life.

The purpose of the summer camp was twofold. First, it afforded us an opportunity to learn technical skills and gain experience in the application of skills we had already developed. Second, we were being watched and rated to determine our strong and weak points, our reactions to the leadership of others, and our potential as officers.

The time we spent was about equally divided between classroom preparation and leadership development

103

through practice. The method of rotation of leadership positions that had been developed gave each of us several opportunities to take charge and accomplish specific goals. The accomplishment of those goals, and the methods we employed served to illustrate our ability to organize, develop responsiveness to our initiations on the part of others, and respond to the initiation of others.

THE FIRST DAY

Frank Simpson came from an eastern university where he was majoring in chemistry. Like many of the other trainees, he had entered the ROTC program to fulfill a mandatory requirement of his undergraduate college. At his school, all students who were physically qualified were required to participate in the first two years of an ROTC program. He voluntarily joined the advanced corps program because he felt that it would enhance his chances of serving his two-year obligation doing more than just menial work. He didn't rule out the possibility of considering the Army as a career, but was not thinking along those lines now. In these respects he was typical of the rest of us.

It didn't take Frank long to get acquainted with the other guys in the platoon. He was convinced that since everyone was in the same situation, they would all be more comfortable knowing each other. Assigned to a lower bunk, he began by engaging in a conversation the fellow assigned to the upper bunk. The fellow "upstairs" was Harry Nelson from VMI, a highly military-oriented college. Harry was accustomed to army life, and knew many of the basic skills required to "survive it." Things like aligning bunks, polishing floors, cleaning weapons, and the like, were second nature to Harry.

Frank, realizing that, like himself, most of the other fellows were standing around trying to figure out what to do with the sheets and blankets issued to them, asked Harry to demonstrate how an army bunk should be made. Although Harry was reluctant to do so, Frank convinced him that he should. Frank spread the word that anyone who wanted to learn should gather around Harry's bunk. Everyone came over to watch, and it wasn't long after the demonstration before they were all involved in conversation. What had been a barracks accommodating 36 silent individuals now became a barracks full of talk and exchange.

104

A little later that day a chart was posted showing the rotation of leadership positions for the six-week period. The assignments ran from 5 P.M. one day until 5 P.M. the next day. Initially Harry was assigned as platoon leader with a rank of second lieutenant, and a fellow named Bob Cramer was assigned as platoon sergeant. Other positions, such as squad leaders, were also assigned. The first task to be accomplished was the preparation of the barracks for an inspection the next morning. Members of the platoon were happy that Harry was their leader because he knew exactly what had to be done and how to do it. Bob was probably the most relieved, since his familiarity with army life was minimal. To most people, the task seemed as insurmountable as it did to Bob.

Harry developed a list of what had to be done and how it was to be done. He had brought along a book used at his school, that specified how things should be displayed and arranged. He had a meeting with Bob, and clearly defined what he wanted done. "This place has to be spotless, and here is a list of things to be cleaned," he instructed. He told Bob that as platoon sergeant it was his responsibility to get the job done. If Bob had any questions, he should refer to the book; and if the answer wasn't there, Harry could be reached at a meeting of platoon leaders at company headquarters. He then set up his personal gear as a demonstration for the others to follow, and left the platoon area.

Bob arranged work details and assigned specific jobs to each group. He tried to organize the work so that each group could avoid interfering with the work of other groups. Obviously certain things had to be completed before others could be started. He made some mistakes, but that was to be expected. Questions arose. When no one present knew the answers, Bob tried to reach Harry but was unsuccessful. Harry's meeting had ended at 8 P.M., but he had not returned. The platoon worked continuously from that afternoon until midnight, when they were informed that it was time for a lights-out and they had to be in their bunks. Harry didn't get back until a little after midnight. He was used to sneaking in after hours and had had plenty of practice at school. He had met a few school buddies at the meeting and "somehow" they became involved in a discussion over a few beers at the PX.

The next day the platoon was awakened at 5:30 A.M. and everyone "rolled" out of bed. In a few minutes everyone heard a commotion going on between Harry and Bob. Harry was yelling something about how the platoon hadn't done any work to clean up the barracks for inspection. He particularly directed the scolding toward Bob, and told him that he had failed to get the job done. This, he said, showed that Bob wasn't much of a leader.

Nobody could understand his irritations. They had worked about twelve hours and thought the place was clean and ready for inspection. Soon the others started yelling back at Harry. He replied that his rating wasn't going to suffer because of their lazy attitude, and that the inspecting officer would be told they refused to do the work assigned to them. He would put the blame where it belonged, that "Bob was an incompetent leader." It was too late to do anything to correct the situation now; the inspection was in twenty minutes. He told the platoon to get dressed and make their bunks.

The inspecting officer arrived on schedule and conducted a thorough inspection of the barracks. He came up with a list of 28 items that were deficient, and told the men they would have six hours to correct the deficiencies before his reinspection. As Harry had said, the place wasn't clean enough.

As soon as the inspecting officer left, Harry pointed out that he had been right and this time he would personally supervise the work so that it would be done. He assigned the jobs to work groups, and continually inspected their progress. Rather than just show them the right way to do things, he criticized their methods and then almost begrudgingly showed them how to do it.

The place was ready for inspection on time. It passed the reinspection.

That evening, Harry was called into the evaluator's office for a review of the day's events. He was asked to appraise what had taken place, and also to evaluate the men under his command. Overjoyed with the opportunity to explain that he was not at fault for the deficiencies of the first inspection, he began to tell the whole story of how Bob had failed.

The evaluator was surprised at Harry's apparent need to defend himself. In fact, the evaluator thought the platoon had done quite well. He complimented Harry on getting the job done as well as could be expected, considering the men's unfamiliarity with Army expectations. He said, further, that he knew the many problems that arise when men are thrown into a situation they have not experienced before. Harry had been put in the leadership position precisely because he had the best chance of accomplishing the task and since he knew what was expected. Harry never mentioned any of this to the platoon. The evaluator also met with Bob and discussed the day. Nothing further was said about the day.

A SYSTEM DEVELOPS

Once it became known that inspection was a daily occurrence, it was obvious that some type of system had to be worked out. The platoon did not have all day to clean because they would be involved in other training programs during daylight hours. The training day typically ended at 6 P.M., and if they spent the rest of the evening cleaning they would have no time for any relaxation, writing letters, or even to prepare for the next day. A system had to be worked out.

Four days passed, during which all their time was spent in cleaning. No matter what they did, it always took as long. The barracks were set up as depicted below.

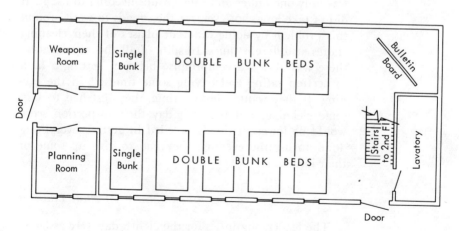

Note: Both the 1st and 2nd floors are identical except only first floor had a lavatory. Area above lavatory (2nd floor) was a "baggage room."

FIGURE 2

barracks floor plan

107

Each side of the room was designated as a squad by the rules of the game. The daily rotation of leadership positions provided for a squad leader who was also a member of the squad. Each squad also had two assistant leaders who were called "fire-team leaders." Fire-team leaders were not in an official leadership position but were chosen by the day's squad leader.

The platoon sergeant was responsible for coordination of the efforts of the squad leaders. His effective use of them would lead to the accomplishment of a mission. The first seven platoon sergeants designated work groups on the basis of squads. Each squad leader was given the responsibility of keeping his area clean, and automatically a line was drawn down the middle of the room dividing it into squad areas. For example, in using the buffer to wax the floor, each squad would wax half of the total floor area. The center aisle was evenly divided. In addition, there were other tasks that had to be performed; the lavatory had to be cleaned; the planning room and weapons room on the first floor had to be cleaned; the stairway had to be cleaned, and the three rooms upstairs had to be cleaned.

On most occasions, each of the four took about the same amount of time. Logically, a squad was assigned to each. Certain problems arose, for instance, because there was only one buffer and four groups needing to use it. It didn't take long, however, for the squads to work around this problem by doing different phases of their cleaning chores at different times. In spite of all this organization there was always a compromise between getting a high inspection rating and having some time off in the evening. If they wanted leisure time, they just had to skip some cleaning. But the next day their inspection score would be lower. If they succeeded in getting everything done during the evening, they had to give up some of their leisure.

A NEW LEADER

The leadership duties for the eighth day were assigned to Sam Carruthers as platoon leader, and Frank Simpson as platoon sergeant. As was usually the case, the platoon sergeant planned and supervised the cleaning operation so as to free the platoon leader to plan his next day's strategy. This time, however, Frank was set on trying something new. He called a meeting of squad leaders and in a short time, with their help, he developed a list of names of people grouped in cliques to which they belonged.

It turned out that there were eight separate four or five groupings of men. Their size closely resembled the size of a fire team, which was a subdivision of the squad. This time he assigned chores to each of the newly recognized groups rather than on the basis of squads. That night, all the cleaning was done and the men still had some leisure time before lights-out. The platoon's rating in the next day's inspection was the highest ever. Consequently Sam and Frank benefited from a higher rating for their twenty-four-hour leadership assignment.

The next day, Harry was again platoon sergeant. The system he used was the one used most often in the past. He set up his work groups in terms of the squad approach.

That night the platoon was again faced with the trade-off problem. They all wanted some leisure time, but for some reason the work was taking longer. Harry, wanting to get the best rating possible, restricted them to barracks until the place was up to his specifications. The platoon did not get the entire job done before lights-out. The next day's inspection rating was not as good.

It was obvious to Harry that the men were working against him. He remembered his first experience, and automatically viewed the situation as one in which the men were trying to get back at him. They had resented his criticism of Bob and his blanket condemnation of their efforts. Frank was more popular, so they worked harder for him. There was no reason why they were unable to get the cleaning done. Harry attributed it all to their lack of cooperation when he assumed the sergeant's post.

Discussion Questions

1. Analyze the background of the various types of students at the camp as to its effect on behavior.

2. In what way did the actions of the first day accurately foretell some of the events which were to occur in succeeding days. In particular, analyze Frank and Harry's behavior on the first day. If you had been at this camp on that day, what would you have predicted from these two in the future?

3. Discuss Harry's behavior as a leader. What were his strong points? Weak points? Would you have liked to have him as a leader? Why, or why not? What type of mistakes, if any, did he make? Why do you think he behaved as he did?

4. What principles of organizational behavior did Frank utilize in his leadership role? Were they effective? Why, or why not?

5. Analyze Harry's behavior after Frank had been leader for one day. What do you think led him to view the situation as he did?

6. What do you think the future holds for Frank and Harry? If you were an officer at this camp, how would you attempt to utilize their various skills?

19

evolution in the mailroom

Anderson Foods, Inc., employs approximately 700 white-collar workers in its administrative headquarters in the southwest.

The mailroom where I worked performs the function of routing incoming and intraoffice mail throughout the building, and dispatching mail to the local post office twice a day.

Hal Struthers, age forty-seven, is the supervisor of the mailroom and has been with the company in that capacity for nine years. He reports to the office manager, Bert Finnely, who is in charge of all office service departments. In addition to the mailroom, these service departments include the reproduction department, maintenance department, and the stationery and supplies department.

Struthers supervises 11 men who carry out the operations of the mailroom. One of these men, Brian Mancies, is his assistant and officially in charge of the mailroom when Struthers is absent. Mancies is twenty-seven years old and has worked in the mailroom for seven years. The work of the department is divided into two principal functions: the circulation of intraoffice mail, and the routing of outgoing mail. The circulation of intraoffice mail is done by four mailboys, each of whom delivers and picks up mail from a single floor. The routing of outgoing mail is performed by three men. One of the men, Carl Peck, is in charge of this operation and reports to Struthers. Peck is fifty-two years old.

At 8:15 A.M. incoming mail was sorted into various pigeon holes arranged by floor. At 9:00 A.M. the four mailboys made their "runs," delivering the mail that was in the pigeon holes to the various offices on their floors.

While on their runs, they picked up mail and brought it back to the mailroom. The runs took about twenty minutes. On returning, they sorted the mail into the pigeon holes and placed any outgoing mail on the worktable of the outgoing section. These runs were repeated every hour on the hour until 4:00 P.M. The intraoffice personnel finished their day at 5:00 P.M. Struthers also finished work at this hour.

The three outgoing men reported for work at 10:30 A.M. They sorted the outgoing mail into various pigeon holes as it was brought to them by the mailboys. The mail was sealed, weighed, and affixed with postage. They also wrapped cartons and packages for mailing as these were sent down by various departments in the company. The work for the outgoing crew ended at 6:30 P.M., when they "closed up shop" and took the mail to the local post office.

All this work was performed in the same room. Although there was a division in the work performed between the outgoing and intraoffice personnel, there were no partitions in the room. The outgoing personnel had their work space in one corner of the room, and the rest of it was occupied by the intraoffice personnel. There were only two desks in the rooms, Struthers' and Peck's. The remainder of the furniture consisted of worktables, pigeon racks, and postage machines. There were chairs scattered in the room for the personnel to use between runs and during slack periods. The work was usually done while standing, although there were no rules requiring this.

Because of this layout, and the nature of the work performed, there was a lot of conversation and socializing. The work essentially required little attention. The relationship between Struthers and his subordinates was very informal, and usually there was considerable joking and bantering going on throughout the day. Struthers was well liked by his subordinates.

In general, the work situation was characterized by informality and harmony. The two work groups in the mailroom engaged in competition and rivalry both on and off the job. A game that often developed between the outgoing and intraoffice personnel was which group could get ahead of the other in clearing mail off their worktables and into the pigeon holes. The winners had first choice of the most comfortable chairs in the room. A similar game was played within the two groups. In spite of the intensity with which this game was played, there was mutual cooperation and "pitching in" in the instances when the workload became too heavy for one group or one individual.

Off the job, too, there was much socializing. It ranged from eating lunch together and pitching horseshoes during the lunch hour, to occasionally getting together and watching a weekend baseball game. Each summer the employees of the mailroom organized an informal picnic which was held at Struthers' home. Generally, all the employees attended the picnics.

In February of my fifth year, a new mailboy was hired to replace one who had been promoted to another department. The new mailboy was Earl Snell. He was twenty-one years old, and had been employed twice before by other companies in the area. He took over the first-floor mail run.

Two weeks after Snell was hired, a change was introduced into the mailroom's operation. A data processing system was installed to handle customer accounts from the billing department. The system consolidated billing procedures, and was able to print out invoices which showed the amount customers owed Anderson Foods. The bills had previously been handled by secretaries who filled them in, placed them in envelopes, and sent them to the mailroom as they finished them. With the new system this tedious and time-consuming procedure was eliminated, and bills could be processed much more quickly. The bills were sent to the mailroom in stacks, where they were then separated into various regions and inserted in envelopes.

Because of the speed with which the machine processed the invoices, they could be handled efficiently only in large amounts. Hence the billing department ran the accounts off at irregular intervals during the day. The result was that the mailroom often received several hundred bills at a time and at irregular intervals. It was not uncommon to receive over a thousand invoices in one day. Extra help was not hired in the mailroom because it was planned that the mailboys could help in separating and stuffing the bills into envelopes during their free time between runs.

From the outset of this new operation, I noticed a change in the atmosphere of the mailroom. The joking and bantering was not so prevalent; on several occasions, when some of the mailboys began joking while sorting the mail, Struthers was quick to tell them to "cut it out and keep your minds on your work."

The new mailboy, Snell, was a constant topic of conversation among the other employees. Snell always managed to be somewhere else when there was work to be done. His runs were never made on time, and he often took as long as an hour to get around on the first floor. Struthers was constantly receiving complaints from other department supervisors that Snell was socializing with the secretaries on his mail run and interfering with their work. When Struthers asked him where he had been and why his run had taken so long, Snell invariably replied, "I had to go to the men's room." Once Snell said to me: "I get a kick out of Struthers. Every time I'm late, I tell him I had to go to the men's room. The number of times I've told him that I've gone to the men's room would have lasted any normal person a lifetime! He is so harmless, though, that even if he didn't believe me he wouldn't do anything about it."

Snell also irritated the other mailroom employees. He often commented that he couldn't wait to get out of the mailroom and into a better job. He couldn't imagine why anyone would settle for a career in such "meaningless" work. One habit of his particularly irritated the other employees. Snell often arrived just after they had cleared off the worktables and dumped another pile of mail on the table. They would complain to him and tell him to clear the table himself. This happened several times, and finally Snell went to Struthers and told him that he was being picked on. Struthers gathered everyone together and gave a "pep talk" about how everyone in the mailroom was expected to cooperate, help each other out. "I like to think of us in this mailroom as a team," said Struthers, "and not as a collection of individuals with individual jobs."

There were several cynical remarks made after Struthers' talk about "team spirit." The favorite expression became "rah, team spirit," when work had to be done. The rest of the employees decided that since Struthers wasn't going to do anything about Snell's lack of cooperation, they would do something about it themselves. The next time Snell arrived late with his mail, all the other employees told Struthers that they had to go to the men's room—and they left. Struthers then took Snell aside and spoke to him privately. After the conversation Snell left the room in a hurry.

Since I was the only one left in the room, Struthers came over to me. "I can't understand that kid. I've tried so hard to reason with him and get him to cooperate. I've gone out of my way to help him out. He only makes trouble for himself the way he acts, and will never get a promotion at this rate. I'm tempted to give him one, just to get him out of my hair! He's making a mess of this whole operation."

Later that afternoon Finnely, Struthers' supervisor, came to the mailroom to find out what was the matter. Snell had gone to him and told him that the employees, including Struthers, were picking on him. Finnely was not ignorant of the situation with Snell, for Struthers had mentioned it to him before. Finnely himself talked to the employees and told them that it was "kid stuff" to do what they had done in the morning. He said that the answer to the whole problem was to concentrate on work and learn to help each other instead of fighting each other.

But the situation didn't improve. Struthers had trouble getting the mailboys to take it on themselves to help with the invoices as they came in. They resented having to stop what they were doing in order to process the invoices when several hundred came in at a time. Often the invoices arrived late in the afternoon, and several employees would have to stay overtime in order to finish them. They couldn't understand why the invoices came in all at once instead of being spread out during the day. Struthers tried to explain to them that the machine could only process several hundred at a time. But this didn't convince them. Struthers himself often commented, "I understand their problems in the data processing, but I wish they would understand mine. There ought to be a better way of doing this. This procedure saves the boys upstairs headaches, but gives a lot of them to me."

The fact that Snell managed to dodge most of the invoice work irritated the other employees. One of them once commented: "Struthers is so gullible. If I were him, I would fire Snell in a second. I can't understand why he doesn't."

About this time Struthers revealed another change. For several months discussion had been going on about integrating some of the activities of the mailroom and the reproduction department, which was adjacent to the mailroom. The reproduction department, like the mailroom, was characterized by periods of intense activity and periods of relative quiet. The initial plan was to have the employees who were not busy in one department assist in the other department if they could be of help. Struthers was very concerned that the mailroom employees should cooperate all they could with the plan.

The cooperation never materialized. The employees suddenly found work which appeared to keep them occupied continuously in the mailroom. One employee was seen to empty the mail out of his pigeon holes and sort it back into them again. The cry was often heard: "Send Snell over to reproduction!" Struthers was upset over the lack of cooperation, and became more and more irritable. He was very concerned because no one was volunteering to help in reproduction, in spite of the fact that on several occasions reproduction had sent men over to the mailroom.

Toward the end of the summer someone mentioned that nothing had been said about the annual picnic. One of the other employees remarked that it was just as well. The lunchtime horseshoe game, a usual summer activity, had never gotten started and nobody ever bothered to play the game of "who could clear the work tables first" any more.

Discussion Questions

1. Describe the jobs of the intraoffice mail personnel and the outgoing mail personnel. In what significant ways were these jobs different?

2. Describe the "games" played by the various personnel in the mail office. Why do employees play such games? What are the positive and negative aspects of these games?

3. Technology affects human relations. Substantiate that statement in the light of incidents taking place at Anderson Foods.

4. What meaning could be attached to the fact that the new mailboy, Earl Snell, and the first organization change occurred very close in time?

5. Why do you think Struthers treated Snell the way

he did? Was this good or poor supervision? Why? What effect did his treatment of Snell have on Struthers' relationship with the other employees?

6. *Why do you think there was so little cooperation given by the personnel in the mailroom to those in reproduction? What group effects could be operating here?*

7. *How would you assess management's skill in running the operations of Anderson Foods, Inc? Do you think Anderson Foods is an efficient organization? Explain your answer.*

8. *The evolution at the mailroom of Anderson Foods has not been beneficial. In what way could the process be redirected?*

9. *Assume that Hal Struthers asks you for his help. What would you recommend?*

20

the job change

The Sarazan Manufacturing Company, leading producer of water meters, is owned and managed by one of New England's oldest families. The company employs approximately 500 people. In the middle 1960's the factory moved from an old four-story building in South Boston to a new modern two-story building in a new industrial center located in Lexington.

Because of the demand for temporary additional help necessitated by the move, four college students were employed as stock clerk's assistants. I was one of these students. Our duties were to organize and pack stock which included raw materials, machine parts, and subassembly parts.

During the period of time I was working at Sarazan I got to know several of the employees quite well. Among these was a fellow named Stan who had been with the company for about seven years. When Stan first started he drove a chisel (fork-lift truck) for approximately a year, but had spent the rest of his time with the company as a stock clerk. In this job he checked incoming stock, prepared production orders, and brought stock to the elevator for delivery to the appropriate department.

His method of handling day-to-day activities was quite simple—and he did his job exceedingly well. The production orders were given to him from the production control office. These orders were always for a specific period of time, usually several days. On the given date for a particular order Stan assembled the materials and delivered them to the various departments. On the rare occasions when a foreman came to the stock room to request some specific material, Stan had them fill in the necessary forms. After he checked out his supply, he called the particular foreman and informed him of how much of what he wanted was available and indicated to the foreman when he would be able to deliver it. Stan felt himself in control of his daily activities, and had the reputation of a very energetic and efficient worker. He was happy and easygoing, and it was a pleasure to deal with him.

As the new plant neared completion, it was learned that additional drivers would be needed to move materials in the new factory. Since Stan had retained his driver's rating, he was sent to Lexington as a driver. This was at the beginning of my third week of employment. One week later I also was transferred to the new plant. When I arrived, I found that there were four chisels, one in shipping and receiving, and the other three under the stock-room foreman's supervision. These three chisels were responsible for (1) moving stock to and between work areas, and (2) arranging stock and stacking pallets in the stock area.

Stan was driving one of these chisels, which was smaller than the other two and could turn in the aisles. Since his truck was also capable of reaching higher than any of the others, he was called on to do odd jobs that could not be done by others.

In his new job Stan was supposed to receive orders only from his boss, the stock-room foreman. But, because of the rush nature of the work on the new plant, Stan often received orders from many other people. While driving through the plant, going to or coming from a particular job, it was not unusual for another worker or foreman to stop him and request that he move something. At the beginning, Stan usually acceded to their wishes even though it often cut into his schedule. As a result of this, Stan was often bawled out by his supervisor for not getting back on schedule from a given job.

When Stan tried to explain the situation, his supervisor said, "Well, who do you think you're working for anyway, me—or those other guys in the plant. You do what I say, and nothing more." After this, Stan would not do the various odd jobs the other foremen requested of him. This often caused conflict with these foremen, for they thought Stan was trying to sabotage their efforts to get their jobs done. When Stan tried to explain what his boss had told him, the other foremen would dismiss this by saying, "Yes, but our main job here is to get operations going as efficiently and as quickly as possible. You've got that special chisel, and you should be helping us no matter what your boss says!"

Despite all this, and knowing Stan's good nature, I had expected to find him relatively satisfied with his new job. After all, he was working at the new plant—which had more prestige than working at the old plant; he had an interesting job in that he was called on to do many different tasks; and because of the job change, his salary had been slightly raised.

To my surprise, however, I found that Stan was a totally different person than the fellow I had known at the old plant. He was sullen, uncooperative, and did less work than he had done as a stock clerk. He would often ignore a request to do a job; and if he did consent he was very impatient and reckless, often banging into things and dropping and damaging materials. He was continuously complaining and would readily associate himself with any group that was currently expressing dissatisfaction. His foreman indicated that unless Stan's behavior improved rapidly he would be dismissed.

Discussion Questions

1. *Stan's behavior differed markedly after his transfer from the old to the new plant. How would you explain this?*

2. *Outline and analyze the interactions Stan had with his co-workers in each plant. What effect would these interactions have on the way he performed his job?*

3. *How would you explain the behavior of Stan's foreman at the new plant? Do you think the foreman's attitude toward Stan would change once the plant became fully operational? Why, or why not?*

4. *Stan undoubtedly had an official job description for the jobs he held at each plant. How do you think these read?*

5. *Do you think that more adequate job descriptions for all the principals involved in this case would have led to a more efficient and harmonious relationship? Discuss.*

6. *Could management do anything to change Stan's job at the new plant so that he would once again become a cooperative and productive worker? If so, what?*

21

barney and
the coding department

During the early 1960's I worked for a large food processing company in their market research department. I worked the night shift from 6 P.M. to 11 P.M., and also all day Saturday.

The work of the night division was essentially the coding of questionnaires sent out by the company. These questionnaires were concerned with various products that were being developed.

The questionnaires were distributed and collected by field representatives, and sent back to the New York Office without any comment or correction by the field representatives. The questionnaires were then turned over to our group for coding. After coding the completed code sheets were sent to the IBM department, where each questionnaire was placed on a separate IBM card. The results of these cards were tabulated and used for future product changes and promotion policies.

The steps in the coding process were as follows:

1. NUMBERING. The questionnaires were numbered with regard to the city where taken and the individual questionnaire number.
2. STAPLING. After numbering, the questionnaire was broken down into as many members of the family as responded. Each member was treated as a separate response.
3. EDITING. Editing involved the checking of the response of the housewife (and family members) to questions concerning factors such as age, income, and members in the family. This was designed to insure that all questions were answered.

4. CODING. After editing, the questionnaires were collected and then given out again for the actual coding. Coding involved the transfer of the responses to separate coding sheets.

These were the four basic processes involved in the coding procedure. They are listed above sequentially without reference to the various intermediate steps which take place. Of these steps, editing and checking were the most important.

Two conferences were held for each type of questionnaire; once for the editing, and once for the coding. These conferences were attended by Barney, the supervisor, and his assistant, Ken, and the people in the night crew who were to work on a particular questionnaire.

Each question and the possible responses to it were discussed. This procedure would have been fine, if the questions had been productive. However, each member felt obligated to ask at least one question, any question, just to take up some time. As a result, these conferences took an inordinate length of time.

The checking process was another important function of the night crew. After a set of questionnaires was either numbered, stapled, edited, or coded it was then checked a second time by a different person. After this second check, a third check was made by still another person. Thus each questionnaire was checked and double-checked a total of eight times (twice after each of the four operations). This, obviously, also took a great deal of time.

Our supervisor Barney was single and in his early forties. He had been with the company for ten years, and in his present capacity for the past two years. He worked from 3:00 P.M. to 11:00 P.M. Barney had found a girl friend, and was dissatisfied with the night-shift hours. This dissatisfaction was evidenced by his frequent one-and-a-half to two-hour breaks during the night. Occasionally he returned from these trips slightly inebriated.

Barney had sole responsibility for the coding process and received little direction from above. He was the center of communications, so far as the night crew was concerned. Unfortunately, Barney had an extremely cold personality. He said little to the men, kept to himself, drank coffee from his private pot all night, never mixed, and rarely smiled. He did not praise the men for achievements, and would often growl at their laxity.

Barney's assistant Ken was about twenty-one and a senior at a local university. Ken was born in Haiti and still spoke with a very pronounced Spanish accent; so much so, that at times it was difficult to understand him. Ken, like Barney, spoke very seldom; but unlike Barney, he was extremely serious about his job. His general personality was unobjectionable except that he liked to appear as the young martyr—the poor struggling student who had to work and be serious about his employment, more so than the rich American boys who worked under him.

One of the aspects of the job which particularly irked the men was the complex rating system used in the company. Each man was rated with regard to his speed and accuracy on each job to which he was assigned, i.e., numbering, stapling, editing, and coding. The assignment to each of these tasks was on a rotating basis. It was important that each man spent equal time on each job. As a result, the time a man spent on each task was calculated down to the minute. Because of this complex rating system, Ken spent most of his time keeping accurate time cards on the progress of each man. About every three or four months, Barney called in each person and told him how he stood in relation to the other people on the night shift.

The way in which the company regarded absenteeism and tardiness was rather unusual. On the one hand, even though absenteeism was quite high it was not considered very serious. In fact, most of the people who were going to be absent on a certain evening did not even bother to call in. On the other hand, tardiness was considered to be very serious.

Everyone was due at 5:50 P.M. If a man arrived before 5:40, he got an extra 35¢ per hour, if he arrived before 5:45, he got an extra 17¢. If, however, he arrived after 5:50, he lost 17¢ for every five minutes he was late! To make matters worse, if he arrived after 5:50, the individual was not allowed to check in on the clock in the lobby but had to check in on the clock in the office, which was on the ninth floor. As a result, he lost an additional five minutes in the elevator. What made this all particularly annoying was that nobody started to really work until 6:15 anyway!

There were a lot of ridiculous rules which everybody followed—because they knew there would be severe penalties if they didn't. For example, no one was allowed to either make or receive phone calls during working hours. This was bad enough; but the "no talking" rule was even worse. No one was allowed to talk during working hours. If someone forgot and spoke to his neighbor he would be disciplined by having his desk moved to a vacant corner in the office for the rest of the shift. I couldn't believe that this was really company policy, but Barney practiced it with a vengeance.

One of Barney's favorite stunts was trying to catch the group off guard. When he returned from his break he would take the elevator to the tenth rather than the ninth floor. This was done so that the bell on the ninth floor would not ring when the elevator stopped. Thus, he could not be heard when he approached. He would then walk down the stairs from the tenth floor to the ninth to see if he could find someone loafing. If he did, this worker was disciplined, usually through a lower rating during the next evaluation.

Despite the foregoing, the workers were not terribly dissatisfied with the job. Turnover was slightly higher than in the rest of the organization, but this did not seem to bother management. Even though not much dissatisfaction was expressed, the workers did not go out of their way to produce. Most of us just viewed the job as part-time work for some extra money. We weren't particularly concerned with how we did the job—or how much we were yelled at—so long as we got paid. If we could pretend to be working and get away with it, fine.

Discussion Questions

1. Rules and procedures are required by all organizations. What kind of rules were used in this one? Do you think the rules were effective? Or rational? Discuss fully. What rules would you recommend for this organization?

2. Why do you think there were such extensive checking and rechecking procedures for each questionnaire? In what way does this reflect on the motivational techniques used by management?

3. What rationale might the company have for its stringent tardiness policy as opposed to its lax absenteeism policy?

4. Was Barney a good supervisor? Why, or why not?

Analyze his method of checking up on the employees, e.g., the elevator technique. What do you think of this?

5. Do you have any cues as to the effectiveness of the top management of this firm? What are these cues?

6. Do you think that the coding department is a place where you would like to work? Why, or why not? What changes would you recommend to make it a better place in which to work?

22

diary of a failure

On January 5, 196–, I began working for a small but well-known firm in public opinion polling. At the time I started this job I had high hopes for a successful career with the firm.

The following chart reflects the organizational setup when I began to work:

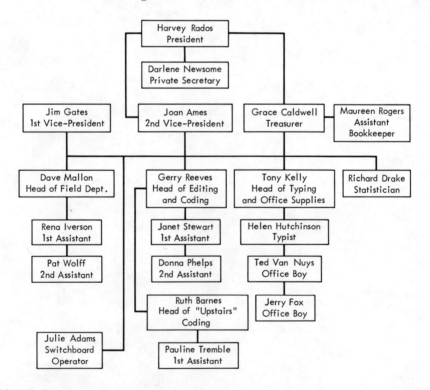

FIGURE 3

organization chart for Rados Research, Inc.

A typical work pattern (best understood by reference to the organizational chart) is described below:

1. A client contact generally initiated with Harvey Rados (President). He submitted a proposal to the client and when it was accepted and partial payment of the project received, the job was assigned a number and work began.
2. Either Harvey Rados himself or one of the two vice-presidents were assigned the "job." In the case of Job Number 2376, we will assume that Joan Ames (Second Vice-President) was put in charge of the job. She would then write a questionnaire, and when it was approved by the client she would call in Dave Mallon (Head of Field Department) and Gerry Reeves (Head of Editing and Coding) and perhaps Richard Drake (Statistician).
3. Drake would pick a sample, and Mallon would consult with him on this to be able to line up Rados Research part-time interviewers in the area. Questionnaires would be printed by Office Supplies, and Mallon would be in charge of mailing them to the proper interviewers and getting them back on time.
4. As questionnaires were returned, Gerry Reeves would accumulate them and assign individuals in coding to "build" codes and finally to code all the questions in the questionnaires.
5. Coded questionnaires were sent to a commercial data processing company which punched them on cards in a manner specified by Reeves and the analyst —who was, in this case, Joan Ames.
6. When the printed "runs" were returned by the data company, Reeves and Ames went over them together to see if more were needed.
7. Ames then took over, compiled charts from the runs, and began her analysis.
8. Ames would write her report and then submit it to Harvey Rados for his approval. When he finished his often extensive corrections, report number 2376 went to typing where it was put in order, typed, mimeographed, and finally mailed to the client.
9. Either Harvey Rados or Joan Ames or both would then call on the client and give an oral presentation of their findings.
10. Copies of the report, the runs from the data company, and the questionnaire, were filed under Job 2376 and the case was considered closed. From start to finish, a job could take two weeks if the firm was rushed. If there was no rush, and the people to be interviewed were many and scattered across the country, the job might take as long as six weeks.

JANUARY 5 First day at work. They say I'm to work in the Field Department for a few weeks to get the feel of the place. Dave Mallon (head of Field) took me to lunch today and we talked about the whole department. He's going on a trip next week to line up interviewers, and in his absence I'll run the department with his assistants.

JANUARY 12 Ran Field Department this past week. Set up a whole series of interviews. Mallon came back today and liked the way things were going—told me I'd done a good job. I told him the assistants let me know what to do, and I did it. I was proud and quite enthusiastic about working for this company.

JANUARY 15 Have been helping Mallon in the Field Department, and reading copies of old reports to get the feel of how to write them up. I've been coming in on Saturdays and getting to the office early to read a lot of them (no reports may be taken home).

(Harvey Rados had pointedly suggested that I read all the old reports I could when he hired me.)

JANUARY 18 Kelly told me I was coming in too early, and that coming in on weekends was bad. He saw me at the office on Saturday while I was reading reports, and he dropped in to pick something up. He said it made the rest of them look lazy. He seemed to be quite a gossip. I told him that I just wanted to learn a lot so I could write a report in the style the company demanded, and that this was important because I had been hired as an analyst.

JANUARY 19 Rena Iverson made a remark that I was "trying to be the next president of Rados, Inc." I just laughed. Decided not to do any more reading of reports on Saturdays or early mornings. It seemed to really upset a number of people in the office. They not only made remarks but also were noticeably cool to me. To keep up with the reading—which I think is vital to the training—I took a few reports home, even though this is against company policy.

JANUARY 20 Joan Ames spoke to me today. She said that Kelly had seen me wth a report in my briefcase. She warned me that Rados didn't like them taken out of the office.

JANUARY 24 Today I was given a chance to run a study from start to finish. I'm writing a questionnaire, and will fly to St. Louis to organize the interviewers. Rados told me that I will be in charge of the whole thing and get a chance to write up the paper although he will deliver it. Sounds good. Looks like I am being accepted around here.

FEBRUARY 9 My study is finished. I was in St. Louis for three days. When I returned to the office and got the data back I went into an empty office, moved an old bridge table and chair in, and wrote up the study. I submitted it to Rados' secretary, Darlene Newsome. Thought I did a good job.

FEBRUARY 12 Grace Caldwell (treasurer and in charge of purchasing equipment) told me I could have that office permanently. She ordered furniture, and helped me arrange it.

FEBRUARY 13 I met Rados in the men's room and he said "Good job," and walked out. It was the first time I had seen him in two weeks. I feel it deserved more than this. I wonder what's going on.

FEBRUARY 16 Jim Gates asked me to come in on Saturday to prepare some statistical tables for a report he was writing. Worked nine hours on Saturday, and finished the tables.

FEBRUARY 18 Darlene Newsome told me that "some disgusting animal" had left a cigar butt in her ashtray over the weekend. I realized it was mine—left there on Saturday when I worked in the office alone. Because I thought she knew it was mine I said, "I'm sorry, Darlene, I was in a rush and didn't realize the cleaning people don't come in over the weekend." She said, "Around here Harvey Rados is the *only* one who smokes *cigars.*"

FEBRUARY 19 Rados called me in and told me that he had been getting "bad reports" about me. This amounted to leaving a cigar butt on Darlene Newsome's desk, and, by implication, using her desk without her permission (although her desk, because of its central location, was used by everyone to do odd jobs on if they were in a hurry). Furthermore, Harvey said that he felt the tables I'd prepared for Gates were laid out poorly (even though I'd prepared them exactly as Gates had directed). Rados then told me he was busy. I tried to explain, but he picked up the phone and motioned me out.

FEBRUARY 24 Joan Ames told me to help out in coding for a few days. I've been picking up batches of interviews in coding and working on them in my office upstairs. Since I'm next to the "upstairs" coding department, Joan suggested that I work there instead of in my office. The upstairs coding group was not part of the power-group and was, in general, antagonistic toward the latter. Therefore I was not too ecstatic about her suggestion.

FEBRUARY 26 While coding today, I noticed a number of interviews that seemed "phoney"—i.e., that the interviewer in Indianapolis, Indiana, had concocted the interviews in her head rather than actually conducted them. This, I felt, was significant, and so did the two members of the upstairs coding group with whom I was working and to whom I showed the interviews. As a matter of fact, they encouraged me to tell Joan Ames about the phoney interviews. Since it was Joan Ames' job, I told her about it. She said I should show it to Dave Mallon, head of Field Department and in charge of interviews. Mallon wasn't in, but his assistant got right on it and phoned long distance to Indianapolis. We immediately discovered that at least five interviews were wholly fraudulent. The people concerned had not been interviewed.

FEBRUARY 27 Joan Ames called me into her office and bawled me out. She said I had gone behind Mallon's back and shown his interviewers to be crooks when it wasn't my job to do so. She said she didn't like my attitude. Ames felt I should leave these matters to Mallon and Reeves (head of coding). When I apologized she added, "You're picking on the wrong people, you know. Mallon knows his business, and so does Reeves. You're too new to be telling them anything." Couldn't help thinking that I *had* told them something . . . *I* had discovered the fake interviews . . . but maybe they just didn't care . . . ? It all seems very unusual.

FEBRUARY 28 I estimate that 10% to 25% of the interviews are fake on a lot of these jobs. I'd be willing to bet

I could prove it with $25.00 worth of phone calls. But I'd better lay low. It is obvious that the power structure wants me to be quiet about it.

MARCH 2   Darlene Newsome told me that Richard Drake (statistician) had been fired. I replied without thinking, "Oh, I'm sorry." She shot back, "Why? Harvey thought he was no good."

MARCH 4   I've been doing mostly coding. Boring work. I have no one to talk to now that the upstairs coders have quit. (Ruth Barnes and Pauline Tremble quit without notice yesterday.) The office seems to be using me as their replacement. This seems odd, for they were getting $65.00 a week as coders, and I'm getting more than double that amount. Of course I can't do twice as much work. Oh, well!

MARCH 20   Harvey Rados called me in to tell me that the codes I've been building aren't very good. I replied that I didn't actually "build" the codes. I used the codes that were built in the past (as ordered by Gerry Reeves) and just recopied them. Rados got mad and said, "I know poor coding when I see it." That ended the discussion.

MARCH 27   Still coding up in my office. Still bored.

APRIL 1   Got a memo from Rados telling me to move into the downstairs coding room and vacate my office. He felt I should learn coding under Reeves' "personal supervision." Reeves is a funny guy. He's absent a lot and never comes in before noon, so you never get any "supervision" anyway. I don't relish working for him.

APRIL 5   Working in the main coding room. Reeves and Stewart never talk to me. There is only Donna Phelps, and she is afraid to open her mouth in front of the other two. Coding is unbearably dull. They give Donna and me all the tough work, and Reeves and Stewart come in late and take two hours out to have lunch with Ames and Mallon just about every day.

APRIL 8   Rados called me in to tell me that he thought my coding had not improved. I asked him what he meant, and he pointed to several of my codes on his desk. I meekly told him that Reeves checked each of my codes and ok'd them one by one before they were used. I said that Reeves had never offered any additions or corrections. Rados just stared at me, and that was that.

APRIL 9 Joan Ames informed me that I was to be sent out in the field to do interviewing. That's a big step down. No one in the office does interviewing except for pretesting or special interviews of some kind. Things are looking bad.

APRIL 15 Still pounding the pavement interviewing every day. Getting fed up. What a career!

APRIL 17 Since Rados is out of town for two weeks, I spoke to Ames about being taken off interviewing. I mentioned that I was never hired as a field worker, and didn't like it. She told me that my interviews weren't good. I said, "Can you be specific?" She told me that if I couldn't interview or code better than I'd been doing, I'd better get ready for six to ten months of practice. I asked her how she knew anything about my codes or if she'd ever seen one. She said she'd "heard" all about them. I wonder why one needs so *much* practice and work in areas in which he is not supposed to be involved in the first place!

APRIL 19 When I dropped by the office today, Mallon asked me how I liked "working with the common people." I looked right through him. He yelled after me that tomorrow I'd have to interview in Paterson, New Jersey. (He was laughing because that meant more travel, and more time lost.)

APRIL 24 Rados flew in unexpectedly. He asked what I'd been doing. I told him I'd been interviewing. He said that he thought I could be more useful. I agreed with him and told him that I enjoyed analysis and report writing, and as I'd done one job successfully, couldn't I be given another? He didn't answer.

APRIL 25 Met Rados in the men's room and asked him when I'd be finished interviewing. He said, "You'd better count on a few months of it." I made up my mind to leave the firm.

APRIL 27 I handed in my resignation to Harvey Rados and left the firm. My "career" lasted less than four months.

Discussion Questions

1. What is really going on here? Whose "failure" is it? Discuss fully?

2. Do you think that the case writer made any mistakes when he first began the job? If so, what were they? Would you have done anything differently? Is there anything that would lead you to question the reliability of his reporting?

3. Was quitting the only viable action this individual could take? Is there anything else he could have done? Can quitting ever be considered the most appropriate response? Under what conditions?

4. What do you think will happen in the future? Will our "misfit" do better or worse? What factors do you think led to his behavior in the organization?

5. Analyze the lateral relationships existing between the various members of the organization. Is there anything about these relationships that would have led you to expect trouble arising within the organization? If so, what?

6. What suggestions would you make to improve the work flow in the organization?

7. Describe the personalities (as revealed in the case) of the following individuals: Harvey Rados, Joan Ames, Dave Mallon, Tony Kelly, Darlene Newsome, and the case writer. What effect did these personalities have on the operations of the company?

23

the old "new" pilots

The following situation developed at a major Fighter-Interceptor Squadron Base centrally located on the East Coast. The squadron was authorized a complement of 80 rated officers and had just received 50 new flying personnel to bring it to full strength. The squadron had been short of qualified crews for the F-94c (a two-place single engine jet fighter). Only 15 crews had remained after a huge turnover. Three months' time was allocated for training the new men.

THE SITUATION

The primary duty of the squadron was the Air Defense of the most populated area of the East Coast. The location was very important to the Air Defense Command since New York, Washington, and Philadelphia were all within the zone of defense of the aircraft. To make the Fighter-Interceptor Squadron one of the best squadrons in the nation, the Air Force had sent approximately 20 pilots from overseas bases to form a hard core of experienced men who would be a real addition to the "old heads" that had not been transferred.

Most of these 20 pilots came from one-place interceptor squadrons. They were in the habit of doing all the flying and radar work alone. These men did not restrain themselves from expressing their feelings about Radar Observers (RO's). They felt that the man flying with them was unnecessary, despite indoctrination statistics which pointed out the greater capability of two-man interceptors. The five other new pilots were fresh from flying schools.

The remainder of the new officers, 25 in all, were the

Radar Observers. Ten of these men were experienced and had come from overseas bases; 15 were fresh out of school.

The new men who had been assigned to the squadron had one thing in common: none of them had requested East Coast duty. Many of those who had been overseas had come from hardship areas; they were supposed to have been granted their choice of base and had not been, and this led to much discontent among the men.

It was in the actual flying, however, that real trouble developed. The F-94c is so designed that although the pilot is in complete command of the aircraft at all times, during the interception he must follow directions. The Ground Control Center positions the planes for their runs on the target; the Radar Observer takes over when he locates the target on the radar. The pilot is supposed to exactly follow the directions of, first, the Ground Control Center and then the Radar Observer. The latter is seated directly behind the pilot, and they communicate with each other and with the ground over the radio set. The pilot has an image on a small radarscope after the target is located by the Radar Observer, but he is not supposed to actually fly the plane at the target image until the last ten seconds. The Radar Observer is supposed to be obeyed until then.

From various reports that were made out after each practice flight it was obvious that most of the new crews were having great difficulty in making good interceptions. The experienced pilots in particular were having trouble. This was unexpected. Much time was spent in the briefing room going over procedures and tactics, but after two and a half months the results were still not up to the standards necessary to make the crews operationally ready.

The squadron badly needed the new men, but did not want to approve them unless they really could perform satisfactorily. The strain was very great on the 15 qualified crews who were performing all the actual "alert" duties. No one was able to understand the true nature of the problem, and—there was only half a month more for training!

Discussion Questions

1. What was really happening in this organization? What went wrong? Who was to blame?

2. What effect did the old "new" pilots have on this

Fighter-Interceptor Squadron operation? Discuss their re-
action to the Radar Observers, and the possible reasons
for it. In what way is this reaction typical?

3. What recommendations would you make to solve
the problem? Be certain that your recommendations are
feasible.

4. What suggestions would you make for changes in
the operation to ensure that this type of situation would
not occur again?

24

the fate
of the underwriters

The Granville Insurance Company is a very large, nationally known firm with offices and subsidiary companies throughout every state. The company offers a complete line of insurance including life, accident and sickness, fire and theft, automobile, marine, commercial, and so on.

Nationally, Granville is broken down into five major zones; each zone office has under its jurisdiction several district offices to which the numerous branch offices report. The zone offices, of course, report to the headquarters or Home Office. One such zone office is located in Westchester County, New York. Its office building also accommodates one of the large district offices. It was this district office with which I was associated as a trainee, primarily in the Underwriting Department.

Essentially the underwriter's job is the evaluation of risks. It is the underwriter who must determine whether or not new business forwarded by the company's agents is acceptable, and whether or not the company wishes to continue to insure those persons or companies who have begun to exhibit unfavorable loss patterns. The underwriter's responsibility is therefore considerable, for the company's money is very directly tied to his judgment. In recognition of this, management pays the underwriter more than any of the other nonmanagerial employees. Of course actuaries earn more, given their high level of professional training, and successful agents can earn more through high commissions. However, aside from managers and actuaries, the underwriter has the greatest prestige.

A life insurance underwriter must study intensely for

several years and then pass rigorous examinations in order to become a Chartered Life Underwriter. Factors such as this have increasingly added a professional status to the underwriter's job. Also the underwriters are considerably older than employees in other departments because of the management's belief that older people are more likely to have acquired the wisdom and maturity which are necessary for good judgment.

Granville's Underwriting Department is located on a large, open floor that is shared with other departments. Those underwriters who have served the company longest were given the presumably more desirable desks along the windows as well as the limited number of telephones which were used constantly. Since automobile insurance accounted for the vast majority of Granville's business, the greatest number of underwriters were also involved in this line. The entire Underwriting Department was under the direct supervision of the two assistant underwriter managers, Mr. Jason Coombs and Mr. Neil Russo.

Mr. Russo had been in automobile insurance underwriting for many years and was, therefore, more directly concerned with the supervision of the automobile underwriters. Coombs had previously been in Life underwriting and devoted most of his time to this and to the other lines. Both men reported to Mr. Hurst, the underwriting manager.

Because the other lines of insurance (not including automobile) required only two or three underwriters each, we shall be primarily concerned with the automobile underwriters. These were broken down into two formal groups: the In Force underwriters and the New Business underwriters; each was composed of between 20 and 25 persons. In turn these were again divided into two informal groups. In the past several years, owing to retirements, firings, and growth, the personnel people had recruited quite a few younger people to be trained as underwriters. The result was that both formal groups were now composed of a younger set and an older set of people, with the older outnumbering the younger by about three to one. The disparity in age between the two groups was considerable, and it was along these lines of age that the informal groups evolved.

The opportunities for informal interaction were rather limited during the working hours, but very much in evidence during lunch and coffee breaks. There did not at any time appear anything that might have been construed as animosity, jealousy, rivalry, or unfriendliness between the two groups. In fact, interactions which occurred were consistently of a friendly and cooperative nature. Certainly, the younger people had more in common with each other than with the older; they might also have been regarded by the older people—as well as by themselves—as being in a subordinate position (informally) since they were in what might have been regarded as an apprentice relationship to the older set.

INTERACTIONS OF THE UNDERWRITING DEPARTMENT

The underwriters interacted with almost every other department. Personnel was important from the standpoint of training and recruiting. Interaction with the Sales force was particularly extensive, with agents constantly trying to "sell" the underwriter on the acceptability of the new business they wanted to put on the books. The Claims people supplied vital data concerning the loss records of those whom the company had already insured. The Services Department supported the underwriters with essential clerical procedures, handling, and so forth. Perhaps Public Relations was the only unit that did not have a directly vital relationship with the Underwriting Department.

New procedures were constantly introduced. Each time a new interaction pattern was developed to accommodate a new procedure, it seemed that a new procedure was introduced which called for a complete revamping of the relevant interaction. Such changes were presented in an arbitrary "you-will-do-this" manner by either of the two assistant underwriting managers or by Mr. Hurst, the underwriting manager. Often there was an attempt to "pass the buck" with comments such as "We're sorry about this, but it can't be helped. Zone wants a more efficient method of expediting New Business handling, and this is how we've decided to do it."

Changes of this kind always included an opportunity to ask questions in case one did not completely understand his part in the newest procedure, but one was never to question the need for the procedure or offer an alternative procedure. Needless to say, the management never approached the underwriters with their problem beforehand; management did not solicit suggestions for its solution from those who were actually engaged in the work.

One such change particularly bothered the underwriters. The Policy Files unit, part of the Services Department, was intimately linked—perhaps more so than with any other area—with the underwriters. Composed of teen-age girls (except for their supervisor) this unit had the primary responsibility of locating the file or files for any given insured, delivering these files to the members of any department that needed them, and later returning the files to their correct storage places. Furthermore, these girls were to keep the files in proper order. This meant that each paper within a file was to be fastened, chronologically, by means of a small metal fastening device on the folder of each file.

Simple as this duty appears, it involved no small amount of time. Many files carried over 100 pieces of paper, IBM cards, letters, forms, and the like, often of varying degrees of legibility. If one of those files came apart through handling, age, negligence, or whatever, it might require as much as fifteen minutes to properly arrange and fasten it again. Those in charge had allowed these files to become sadly neglected in this respect. It was estimated that approximately 25% of the files were badly in need of attention. (The office contained about 800,000 files.)

One day Mr. Coombs and Mr. Russo called a meeting of the underwriters and informed them that henceforth it would be primarily their responsibility to see that no file ever left their desk without being first checked for the required chronology and attachment. If a file was in need of such attention, the underwriter was to provide it. Coombs and Russo admitted that the formal responsibility for such work was still actually the girls' in the Policy File unit; but in view of these girls' apparent irresponsibility, disregard, and lack of interest, they felt that the more responsible underwriters ought to perform this duty. There was much resentment because of this change; the underwriters felt that they were not being paid to do "high-school kids'" work.

Another change of some importance concerned the training of the relatively large group of younger people in the department. Formerly a new underwriting trainee was left almost solely to his own devices; his training consisted entirely of on-the-job, catch-as-catch-can experience.

However, management now felt that a certain amount of more formalized training was called for to complement the still existing on-the-job training. With this in mind a few of the older and more experienced underwriters were relieved of their ordinary duties twice a week, and told to conduct a class composed of several trainees.

It is interesting to contrast this training program with those in such major departments as Claims and Sales. In the case of these two departments, the training program had been conducted solely under the auspices of the Personnel Department. For years, Personnel had conducted formal classes—with full-time instructors—in these fields. Class sessions lasted all day for a number of weeks. With the exception of short speeches by various key personnel, Claims and Sales people were never actively involved in these training programs. The reason offered for the dissimilarity in these two training procedures was that that Underwriting unit had never had as great a number of personnel that required training as did the other two departments.

For some inexplicable reason, the entire Underwriting Department was moved to another area on the floor—an area that was considerably more remote from other departments than the original location. Previously the underwriters had been in an area bordered on one side by the Claims people, with whom considerable interaction was necessary, and on the other side by the crucial New Business units which received work and instructions in a constant stream from the underwriters.

Underwriting now found that the only unit with which it had face-to-face contact was the Touring Service unit. But with this unit they had no need for interaction. The result was an increase in misunderstandings in the interactions with Claims and New Business as well as a need for *more* interactions to straighten out these misunderstandings. Interaction with other units on other floors was also impeded by the fact that there were not as many phones in the new area as there had been in the previous area. Mr. Hurst promised to have this situation corrected; but as of three months later, no action had been taken.

The changes in management which occurred during this period also caused other problems. Originally Mr. Hurst was the underwriting manager; and there was only one assistant manager, Mr. Barry Thorson. When Mr. Thorson was promoted, it was announced that Mr. Russo, who had been in underwriting for many years and who had just completed the company's Management Training Program, would take his place. It was further announced that Coombs, who had been hired from another company and was still in the Management Training Program, would, on completion of the program, join Russo as a second assistant manager. It is worth mentioning that when Russo was selected for management training, most of the other underwriters felt that another underwriter, Mr. Rankin, would have been a better choice. There was a definite stereotype as to what an insurance executive should be in the Underwriting Department, and Mr. Russo did not correspond to this stereotype.

Neil Russo had been with the company for many years, though no longer than Mr. Rankin and for a lesser period than several others. He had never been to college as had most of the underwriters, particularly the younger ones. It was said that his speech was far from "polished," and at times even somewhat crude; and his manner of dress was, in the opinion of many, "flashy" and certainly not in the conservative vein they would have preferred to see. Many held similar reservations concerning the bright red sports car he drove. Coupled with the facts that he was unmarried, not a homeowner, and not a churchgoer, these observations were sufficient to convince the underwriters that Russo presented anything but the proper image. In his favor was the fact that he tried hard, when approached, to be friendly.

Mr. Coombs, when he arrived, turned out to be quite different from Russo. A conservatively dressed, college-educated person, he drove a black sedan, was noted to be more refined of speech, was married, and to complete the antithesis he was also a deacon at a local church. If one observed his interaction with his subordinates, however, quite another facet of the man would have been revealed. Interactions were few and almost always initiated by the subordinate. Coombs's speech was short and to the point, without a display of emotion. Most of the underwriters expressed the opinion that Coombs was "quite difficult to get to know."

Perhaps management itself held certain reservations concerning these two men. So far as was known, the installation of more than one assistant underwriting manager was unprecedented in the history of the zone. Furthermore, at the time the decision was made, it was generally known that certain executives had alleged that the reason for doing so was that both men were "relatively inexperienced."

During the time that these events were taking place, management found that Underwriting's production had suffered to a large degree in terms of total output and in terms of output per man-hour. Concurrent with this finding, management was informed by Personnel that a recent survey had revealed that morale in the Underwriting Department of the district office was at an extremely low level and was, in fact, lower than any other underwriting department in the country at the time.

Management decided to attack the former dilemma on two fronts, with a third measure to be utilized if necessary. First, the Personnel department was instructed to carry out an extensive recruiting campaign to hire more underwriting trainees. At the same time a former practice —much disliked by the underwriters—was again instituted in the Underwriting Department. At certain times of the year—notably in the late spring and again toward the very end of the year—people in the insurance business are unusually busy with an inordinate amount of paper work. The underwriters, and particularly those in the In Force unit, are especially deluged by the increased burden.

From time to time in the past, during these peak production periods, the underwriters had been "asked" to work overtime to handle this load. Their compensation for doing so amounted to $2.50 for "supper expenses." As salaried employees, they were not entitled to any overtime payments. Most of the trainees, however, were still employed on an hourly basis, and did not as yet enjoy the status of being on salary; consequently they received full remuneration for their overtime work.

Although management was aware that the underwriters deeply resented this practice (many had placed alternative suggestions in the company's suggestion box in the past) it was instituted anyway.

A third line of attack was held in reserve. Other district offices had been contacted to determine if any of these might be able to "loan" our district office some of their underwriting personnel to aid our Underwriting Department during this period. Those district offices which were reasonably close and had anything even re-

143

motely resembling a surplus of underwriters were told by the zone office to stand by. This third alternative was never utilized.

Management did not seem to do anything concrete about trying to alleviate the morale problem. Actually management did not particularly seem to care about the morale of the underwriters. Morale was so low that our turnover rate was one of the highest in the company. Among those who left voluntarily was Mr. Rankin, the underwriter who had not been promoted at the time Russo was selected for Management Training. About a month after Mr. Rankin left, our manager Mr. Hurst turned in his resignation. It seemed to me that the handwriting was on the wall—the Underwriting Department was simply not a very favored one in the organization— so I quit in order to find employment in a more harmonious atmosphere. From what I hear from some of my old friends who are still working at Granville, things have continued to deteriorate since I left. I am certainly glad that I got out!

Discussion Questions

1. Describe the pattern of initiations between the Underwriting Department and the other departments. What effect does initiation have on perceived status within an organization?

2. What do you feel is the status of the underwriter in this organization? Why?

3. In what way did management introduce change to the underwriters? What effect did this have? If you were a manager in the Granville Insurance Company, would you have introduced the changes differently? If so, how?

4. When Mr. Coombs and Mr. Russo informed the underwriters that they would now be in charge of checking the policy files, what, in fact, were they really telling this group vis-à-vis their relationship to other groups in the organization? What different alternatives might have been considered to deal with the policy files problem?

5. Structural changes affect behavior. What evidence do we have for this statement in this case?

6. How would you assess the new training program undertaken in the Underwriting Department? What assumptions were being made about training in setting up this program? Would you have recommended something different? If so, what?

7.   Do you think that the underwriters' objections to Mr. Russo were valid? Why, or why not? To what extent is the proper image important in a job?

8.   What do you think of management's action in asking the underwriters to work overtime with a minimal compensation for "supper expenses"? What effect would this have on the underwriters? How would this affect their relationship with other groups in the organization?

9.   Unless changes are made, what do you think the future holds for the Underwriting Department of the Granville Insurance Company?

10.   What changes do you think should be made in the management of the underwriters at Granville Insurance? How would you implement these changes? From what position in the management hierarchy would you most like to implement these changes? Discuss fully.

25

trouble at
the loading docks

Quality Merchandise, Inc., is a comparatively new entrant into the mail order business, offering a relatively complete line of consumer goods. The corporation has expanded rapidly through acquisition and merger, and at the present time gross sales approximate $160 million per year. Although expansion occurred rapidly, the firm has kept its facilities centralized at one location. Many of the company structures are very old and have forced some adaptation of company needs to existing facilities.

Department 300 of Quality Merchandise is basically concerned with the loading and unloading of company merchandise from trucks. The truck docks and adjoining work areas for the loading and unloading of these trucks are located in one of the older company buildings which is utilized primarily for inventory storage. As merchandise is requisitioned for shipment, the goods are taken from the appropriate area and sent by conveyor from the packers to the loaders to preassigned trucks. There are approximately 30 to 40 trucks in the docks at any one time; approximately half are loaded while the other half are unloaded.

The dock area is partitioned off to match these particular conflicting functions. We are concerned only with the area utilized for the loading of trucks. This particular area of the department employs approximately 25 to 30 people. To facilitate in understanding the physical layout of the department, a work flow and organization chart are given below.

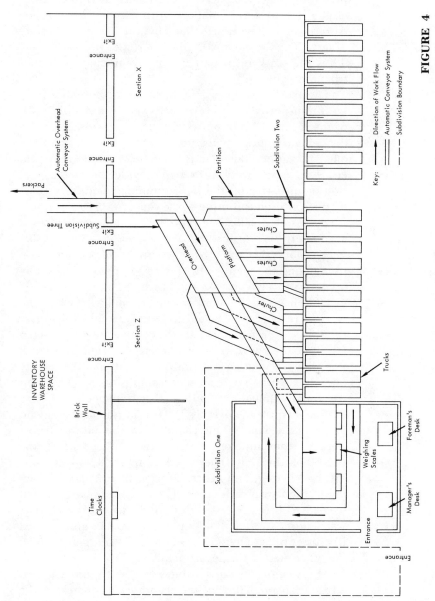

FIGURE 4

work flow and organization structure of department 300.

147

As can be seen from this diagram, the area under study has been redivided into three basic subdivisions. The diagram also shows that work for area Z was initiated by the preceding stage, the packers. The loaders had to continually adjust to a rate of flow instituted by the packers. Also, it should be noted that physical barriers virtually isolated area Z from area X and the rest of the warehouse. Thus the workers in part Z were completely separated from everyone else.

The trucks are loaded by hand, once the goods have been transported by conveyor belts and chutes to the back of the trucks. In the course of a day, each worker on the docks loads approximately two to three trucks. The work offers no variety. Boredom is widespread among the workers. The opportunity to exercise any degree of imagination or initiative on the job is minimal; both are stifled by the continuous routine of the conveyor belt. Each man is responsible for loading procedure so long as he does it adequately. While loading a truck, each worker is basically alone; his truck becomes his world. Communication among the men is infrequent. Social contact usually occurs only during breaks and lunch.

Efficiency was low and became even lower when the workers realized they would have to respond to the same rate of flow even under adverse summer heat. The men felt as if they were getting nowhere. As soon as a truck was filled, the worker was confronted with another empty one. There was no sense of accomplishment. The men continually thought of finding other employment.

The men on the overhead platform (see figure 4) who directed the flow of merchandise to the proper trucks were in constant contact with each other during the course of the day. They worked together, spent their breaks together, and generally were in continuous communication with each other. The overhead-platform men seemed to bring a better disposition to work each day, were more jovial individuals during work, and seemed less susceptible to tension or irritation in comparison with the other men in the department.

Absenteeism and/or tardiness frequently unsettled an already irregular flow of merchandise and increased the overall work burden. Each subdivision of part Z was given a break at a different time, starting with area three. These three different break times in the morning and afternoon varied daily depending on the intensity of the flow of merchandise and occasionally they overlapped. Management would occasionally break everyone at the same time, but usually the process was haphazard.

Another major source of trouble and inefficiency in the department concerns the work originated by the women operating the scales (see figure 4). They are the only workers in the department working partially under a piece-rate system. If they can turn out more than a predetermined amount per hour, as established by management, they then qualify for a bonus adjusted to that amount in excess of the predetermined standard. The hourly rate, or possible bonus, is determined by calculating the daily average. Management considered this system a good incentive to insure adequate output by the women. However, the opposite occurred in reality. The rate was dictated to them by the management without their consultation, and experience showed that it was so high that it was almost impossible to achieve a bonus rate. Although the women were capable of working fast enough to exceed the hourly standard, the flow of merchandise was so erratic that one good hour of productivity was offset by one of inadequate material. The erratic flow of goods never allowed them to pace themselves. They could never be sure how fast or slow the merchandise would come down the conveyor belt, and they could never know whether or not it was physically possible to maintain a "bonus rate" that day. If the women thought they could maintain a "bonus rate" during the course of the day, they would weigh the items as fast as possible.

Thus during periods with an intensive flow of merchandise they completely swamped the men working on docks one and two. This factor would cause much friction and flaring of tempers between the two groups. However, if the girls miscalculated the day's total flow, they exhausted themselves and the loaders—all for nothing. This factor caused further bad feelings between the women and the loaders. Occasionally the flow of merchandise from the packers would be so heavy that to keep the belt from backing up with goods the women had to work as fast as possible. Again the loaders would berate them, the management, and complain about the job in general.

Eventually the women began to ignore the company's bonus incentive and started to establish their own pace. However, in the periods of heavy flow, the manager was there to apply pressure on them to clear the retaining chute and prevent a backup of merchandise on the work belt. Once, under conditions of heavy flow and managerial pressure, a woman completely disregarded the weight of each package as indicated by the scale and applied any postage she chose so that she could turn out the work as quickly as possible. These packages were loaded and shipped out. The shipper discovered the extreme errors in postage, and returned the entire load to Quality Merchandise. They also sent officials back to the mail order concern to investigate and complain. The woman thought to be the cause of the trouble was shortly thereafter transferred to another department.

Another problem that arose several times each week was when the manager or foreman came around to take a loader away from trucks one and two. This left only one man on truck docks one and two, and when the flow of merchandise became intense these two remaining men literally worked themselves into the ground. Needless to say, tempers flared and the remaining workers became even more incensed. As a result one loader rebelled and only filled the back half of the truck, making things much easier on himself. Although this might seem comical, it was actually quite dangerous. With a half-filled truck the weight would shift on curves, seriously endangering the driver and the equipment. The shipper who owned the trucks in question and hired the drivers, again complained that their drivers and property were being endangered. Again the manager and department were subjected to an investigation and embarrassment. The worker involved was sent to a different area in the department.

Late one summer, the company and the shipper decided to install a camera to take pictures of each package before it was loaded onto a truck; this enabled both concerns to have a record of to whom the package was sent, when it was sent, and for how much it was sent. Management thought there was a need for this information, but the means of obtaining it was cumbersome at best. The workers on the trucks found their work much harder and their pace slowed down, thus making it far harder to handle a rush. It turned into a symbol of management authority over the loaders. None had been consulted about the change, and no one ever seemed to care if it made the workers' jobs any harder. Again in rebellion, the workers started taking pictures haphazardly, let parcels go by unphotographed, or photographed the package but not the label for which the camera was intended.

Discussion Questions

1. Contrast the jobs of the loaders, the overhead-platform men, and the weighers. What factors led to the feelings of members of each of these groups? Which of these groups do you think had the higher status in the organization? Which the lower? Why? What are some of the organizational manifestations of perceived low status? Did you see any of these in this case?

2. Assume that you were hired as a consultant by this firm to reorganize their loading dock operations. What suggestions would you make? Outline carefully your approach to the problem and indicate the effect the reorganization would have on the loaders, the platform men, the weighers, and the packers.

3. Do you think that the piece-rate system for the women who weighed the parcels was a good idea? What were the effects of this system? What other type of incentive system could management have initiated?

4. What effect did the initiation by the women weighers to the loaders have on the latter? Why is this?

5. What type of disciplinary system did Quality Merchandise have? Would you consider this to be effective? If not, what would you suggest?

6. Outline the various ways the workers rebelled against the rules of the company. What do you think caused these actions? Is this rebellion a natural aspect of modern society and therefore management could do nothing about it? Why, or why not?

7. Many of the rules and procedures set up by Quality Merchandise were either circumvented or totally ignored. Is it therefore true that there is no place for such rules in a modern organization? If not true, then what is the place of rules in an organization?

26

growth at shamrock

The Shamrock Insurance Company is an international finance organization based in London. Although no formal organization chart exists for Shamrock (appropriately referred to by its initials, SIC) the following is a close approximation based on observation:

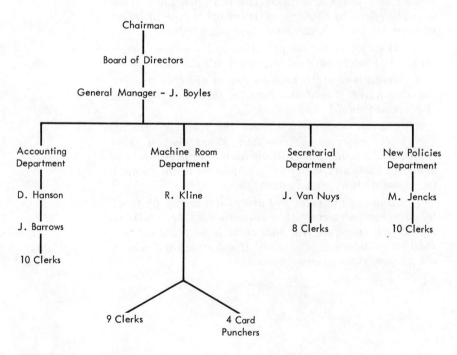

FIGURE 5

organization chart for Shamrock Insurance Company.

The organization had mushroomed over a period of two years from an overseas branch employing five persons to look after the private investments of a millionaire family in South Africa, into the head office of an insurance company that had a turnover of more than $3 million and extended over four African territories. The new organization comprising a staff of over 60 people had been absorbed into the original office system without any serious attempt at planning and coordinating an organization structure.

Except for the computer department (which had been in existence for only a year) all departments were under the management of employees of long standing. It was virtually axiomatic that any new personnel, even if they were involved in technical or specialized work, were subordinate to the senior members of the organization. If the type of work in each department had remained the same, this policy might have been successful. But the scope and volume of work in the accounting, secretarial, and new policy departments required officials with specialized knowledge and skill which the senior employees did not have.

Mr. Van Nuys, head of the secretarial department, was in his sixties, and had obtained his degree at the Chartered Institute of Secretaries some thirty years previously. He had set up a daily routine of doing as much work himself as possible, and delegating very little. He was eagerly looking forward to his retirement in the next few years, but trained no one to assume more of his responsibilities. He made little effort to coordinate the work of the clerks in his department. As the work flow in his department increased, he seemed to hand it out indiscriminately. All the clerks in his department were doing the same type of work, and continually clashed over the need for the same books and voucher files.

Mr. Hanson, who overnight had found himself in charge of an eleven-man accounting department did not possess the tools of either accounting or management. He had been the bookkeeper of the organization for the past twenty years, a post that had led to his dealing with the personal financial needs of the family. The chairman, a member of the family, had pressured Mr. Hanson into becoming a personal lackey to see to such tasks as ordering and collecting airplane tickets, meeting different members of the family at airport and harbor terminals, sending countless telegrams at a nearby post office, drawing up schedules of "latest figures" (which subsequently were found to be hopelessly inaccurate) and so on. When the organization was small, Mr. Hanson had possessed both the time and the ability to complete these duties; now he had neither.

Consequently the responsibility of running the accounting department had, practically speaking, fallen on Mr. Barrows, an extremely hard-working, conscientious, mild person. He lacked the overall knowledge necessary to control the writing up of the books of accounts, and was therefore consistently under pressure from his superiors and subordinates in supplying answers to accounting queries. His mild manner and his inability to exercise authority created a feeling of inadequacy and lack of confidence among the ten clerks in the accounting department. He failed to explain clearly to his subordinates their exact duties and how these duties should be accomplished.

The head of the machine-room department, Mr. Kline, had drifted into machinery control without any formal education in this field. A "good talker" and having a pleasing personality, he had sufficiently impressed Mr. Boyles, the general manager, to be offered the position of head of the computer department. He was not able to delegate the work successfully, nor interested in overcoming the problems that existed in his department. However, his exceptionally successful human relations skills had earned him the confidence of his superiors, namely, the general manager and the board.

INTERACTION BETWEEN ACCOUNTING AND MACHINE ROOM-DEPARTMENTS

The day-to-day interaction of the members of the accounting department under the control of Mr. Barrows and those of the machine room under Mr. Kline is reflected in the following diagram:

Copy deposit slips and vouchers were received about three times weekly through the mail from the branch offices in the four African territories. These vouchers detailed all premiums, dividends, and other income received and deposited in the branch bank accounts. It was the responsibility of the machine-room clerks to analyze

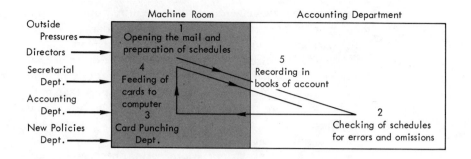

FIGURE 6

machine room and accounting department interactions.

the information in schedules which would be used to punch cards for the machine. The schedule contained the following details: policy number, name of policyholder, date, amount received, type of policy. The assistance of Mr. Barrows and other members of the accounting department was frequently necessary to complete the schedules because of errors and inefficiencies in the card-punching department. After a time it became the practice for all schedules to be checked by the accounting department before they were forwarded to the machine room for card punching.

Four clerks were responsible for the punching of the cards and handing the punched cards to Mr. Kline who then would see that the cards were fed into the computer for updating the premium records. At the end of the run, the total of the premiums updated in the computer was compared with the total on the premium schedule (from which the cards had been punched) and any difference accounted for.

Once a month the machine-room clerks extracted a summary from the computer of the total premiums, dividends, and other income received during the month. This they handed over to the accounting department for incorporation into the books of account.

Since the computer's memory retained the basic financial record of the Company's business, i.e., the amount and date of the last premium paid on each policy, it was important that the day-to-day transactions of the organization flow smoothly and quickly. In addition, all sections of the organization, secretarial, legal, accounting,

155

and upper management, regularly required up-to-date information on premiums recovered in order to answer queries and/or information requests from clients.

A vital requirement of the system, therefore, was that all records be kept up to date and in an orderly fashion for easy reference. Some of the major features that mitigated this were the following: the limited technical and managerial skill of the lower management; lack of a formal organization structure that would assign individual specific jobs; insufficient coordination between departments; the two-week turnaround time for any queries addressed to the branches (i.e., it took at least two weeks to receive a reply from one of the branches in Africa); the approach of the chairman and board of directors who persisted in pressurizing the lower management into providing results, without themselves becoming involved in lower management's problem; lack of recognition given by upper management to those few employees who consistently worked overtime in an attempt to ease the backlog of work; and the general air of boredom, noninvolvement, and disinterest that pervaded most rank-and-file members.

OPERATIONS WITHIN THE MACHINE ROOM

In any exercise where the recording of data is the main administrative goal it is vital that the information should be recorded systematically and regularly. In the machine room neither of these occurred. The lack of a satisfactory system could be traced to the insurance administrative manager of the group in South Africa who had been responsible for the installation of the computer and had left before the system was finalized with the familiar words, "make the necessary arrangements concerning the system."

Before long, this department fell behind with its work. The clerks, mainly single girls under the age of twenty-five, used the inefficiencies of the system as an excuse for their poor performance. The three clerks who had assumed the major roles agreed with Mr. Kline that overtime work was needed and a shift timetable was arranged. Mr. Kline took the night shift from 11 P.M. to 8 A.M. However, the first night the computer broke down. Knowing very little about the technical operation of the machine, Mr. Kline was unable to correct it. The following morning it was learned that he had made no headway. The fault was readily corrected by one of the junior members of the machine room.

The following week Kline persuaded the general manager to allow him four days off to paint his home, with the understanding that the backlog would be wiped out. When the knowledge of this special permission leaked out it was the cause of much annoyance and vexation among the staff. Additional irritation arose over the Christmas bonus allotted to various employees. Mr. Kline received a higher bonus than the managers of the other three departments; it was understood that he was involved in "the most difficult and technical work" of the corporation. The department heads voiced no protest, but the rank and file discussed the imparity openly.

THE COFFEE BREAK SITUATION

It had been the practice for the employees to take coffee breaks at 11 A.M. and 3 P.M. daily in a coffee shop on the street level in the same building. This disruption from work, which usually lasted half an hour, had a detrimental effect on efficiency which the upper management decided to counter. An automatic coffee machine was installed on the second floor to serve the beverage needs of all the organization members.

This machine's product was insipid and unappetizing, and before long the management instructed their secretaries to brew a separate pot of coffee for their exclusive use. When the rest of the staff requested permission to do likewise they were refused, a move that caused ill feeling and resentment. Finally the management was pressured into giving tacit permission for private coffee brewing. By this time, however, numerous staff members had taken to meeting at the vending machine for a social chat while consuming a seemingly unlimited supply of coffee—tokens were being distributed so liberally that there was no limit on the number of "free" cups allowed per person.

What began as a genuine attempt by management to improve efficiency resulted in an equivalent time loss, an increased money cost, and employee dissatisfaction greater than before. Management's high-handed method of dealing with the coffee-break situation had provided their subordinates with a talking point which symbolized their grievances and dissatisfaction.

Although the coffee-break incident might appear to be a relatively minor one, it was symptomatic of the deteriorating conditions at Shamrock. Not only was management unable to effectively run its business operations, but it also seemed woefully inadequate in the effective management of its own personnel.

Discussion Questions

1. Growth is often difficult to control effectively. How did Shamrock manage its growth? What problems did it encounter? What do you think caused these problems?

2. Analyze the lateral relationships between accounting and machine-room departments. Describe any trouble spots that exist. What would you suggest as a way of handling them?

3. Trace the development of the coffee-break situation. What would you suggest to improve the situation? In what ways were management's actions in the coffee-break situation typical of problems in the whole organization? Explain fully.

4. Assume that the chairman of the board of Shamrock, realizing the severity of the situation, decides to hire you as an outside expert to make suggestions about the operation of the company. What would you recommend? Be sure to discuss the operational implications of your recommendations.

27

conflict at a research and development laboratory

This case is about a series of changes made in an engineering services division over a period of some fourteen months. This division was one of fourteen divisions in a large federal government research laboratory. The thirteen other divisions were engaged in basic and applied research, and the Engineering Services Division, as it was called, was actually part of the Administrative Services Division which provided service functions for the research divisions.

Within the Engineering Services Division, there were four branches: the Engineering Design and Drafting Branch, the Production Analysis and Planning Branch, the Mechanical Shop Branch, and the Electronic Services Branch.[1] Primarily we are concerned with the Engineering Design and Drafting Branch.

The Design and Drafting Branch was divided into three design sections—A, B, and C, two drafting sections, and one checking section. Altogether there were some 50 people in this branch.

Within Engineering Services the men knew each other well; many of them played golf together, advised each other not only about technical matters but also about social and personal matters, and frequently did favors for each other.

---

[1]Hereafter, the Production Analysis and Planning Branch will be called the Planning Branch, and the Mechanical Shop and Electronic Branches will be called the Production Branch.

The work of the division was to design, develop, and build models, mechanisms, and instruments for use by scientists in their experiments in the research divisions. The devices varied enormously in purpose, from high precision-measuring equipment to large support structures. Most of the devices were constructed only once; however, continuous modifications and refinements were made to many of them as required by the changing needs of the experimenters.

Requests for engineering or production services normally originated in the research divisions. The requests went to the Planning Branch, which sent those needing engineering services to the Design and Drafting Branch. Generally the remaining requests that could be met without engineering services were handled by the Planning Branch.

In acting on the work requests sent to them, the Design and Drafting Branch would contact the Research Division, try to determine the experimental requirements and acceptance boundaries, and then develop working designs and drawings to build the equipment.

However, in the development of a design and working drawings, a great many alterations were made in order to include additional experimental requirements and accessory equipment or to provide better accessibility or easier machinability.

Scientists and designers started many alterations. However, many alterations were also started by people in the Production area. They were initiated by different levels and at different times, depending on the nature of the changes. For example, sometimes these alterations involved a different sequence of finishing and coating operations that production thought would be easier to handle, or which would result in a better product; this might have been pointed out by an electroplating worker, or a leadingman.

Many designers went to see particular machinists several times a day to discuss progress on a project. Frequently alterations were made on the spot. It was essential for most designers to be able to do this; otherwise, the amount of work that would be required in going through the official channels—making changes in drawings, sending them through checking, through planning, and then through the master mechanic, chief quarterman, and on down—would have caused a virtual standstill in production. This system of communications was not always embraced wholeheartedly by everyone, but was accepted because it usually worked without conflicts and disagreements.

It was because of this necessity for frequent alterations that much interaction took place, especially between designers, draftsmen, and production. Although no one liked to alter what he thought was complete, almost everyone recognized that constant modification was part of the work.

The checking and drafting people worked within Engineering Services Division building most of the time, but the design sections had quite different patterns of work from the drafting and checking groups, and also among themselves. One design section (Section A) almost always stayed at their desks, or at least within the building. This was attributable to the very strong personality of their supervisor, who watched their work and work habits very closely. In another section (Section B) conditions varied. Some men worked for months or years with a research division, and had a room in the other division for themselves; others in that section usually worked at their desks. In the third section, where I worked, the situation again was different. The designers worked at their desks, but they also made frequent trips to the research divisions during the day. This section (Section C) also had more contacts with people in the Production shops and with Planners.

Designers, and, to a certain extent, draftsmen and production personnel often identified closely with a project and helped in setting up experiments. They shared with the scientists the tense excitement of throwing on switches, gradually but inexorably bringing a variety of instruments into operation, and intently watching dials and gauges for the first indications that a new device was working. Not infrequently designers would go out on field trips with scientists, attend their meetings, and have lunch with them. In these instances, the relationship was informal and friendly with a mutual exchange about progress and bottlenecks. Many of these designers became familiar with future experiments being planned as well as with the functioning and capabilities of other equipment in use in the laboratories. They often suggested changes and alterations, which many times resulted in additional requests being issued by the research division.

Many projects were expanded in this way, and for the scientists and the designers this insured continuity of relationships. Those divisions that submitted requests only sporadically could not always be assured of fast service. Designers were reluctant to break away from comfortable relationships with scientists they had come to know well; and scientists were reluctant too, since they could not be sure when they could get design services again, or whether they would have to explain their work to an unfamiliar designer.

CHANGES IN THE ENGINEERING SERVICES DIVISION

At this time, and throughout the period covered in this case, there was a great emphasis in the government on cost savings. Posters, leaflets, and stickers with "WOW" (War on Waste) were placed in every building, on many doors, on most bulletin boards, and in other conspicuous places. Cost savings permeated discussions and practically all activity. This was especially noticeable in the Engineering Services Division, and coincided with the arrival of a new manager from another federal government activity.

The new manager came to the laboratory to head the Engineering Services Division in July 1968. In contrast to the manager who had just left the new manager was a cigar-brandishing, aloof fellow who impressed most people as being definitely unfriendly. From the grapevine it was learned that the new manager had been "successful" —nobody knew how successful—in instituting a series of changes in the production operations of another government—but nonresearch—activity. Hence many people were apprehensive when he asked for a report about the status of all work and available manpower. A great flurry of activity took place as people attempted to find out what was to be included or excluded from the report, and what the report was to be used for. Nevertheless, the report was somehow put together and turned in.

THE AUGUST CONFERENCE

In August 1968, the new manager called the Design and Drafting Branch, and the Planning and Production Branches (in separate conferences) to discuss a new promotion policy and a new arrangement of personnel. The promotion policy for the Design and Drafting Branch included the establishment of "super" grades for those who "excelled" in their work, and also a sort of journeyman level for other designers and draftsmen. Other positions were to be added in which the personnel were not going to report to the chief engineer but directly to the manager. Specifically, a staff of industrial engineers and a staff of project engineers were to be added.

It was explained that Design would now not have to worry about coordinating projects between scientists, planning, and production, but could for the present remain at the board and do what they were "best suited to do," that is, design. The project engineers were to act as "quarterbacks—carrying the ball between scientist and designer, designer and planner, and designer and production problems, and so forth, between groups."

The industrial engineers were to conduct studies—the exact subjects of which were unclear, although everyone "knew for certain" that industrial engineers made work measurements and methods studies. The implications were obvious, and this generated much discussion and anxiety. One very important point should be made: the manager was normally rotated in his assignment to other facilities every two years, so that there was a definite period of time in which the new manager had to act and accomplish things. People were conscious of this, and it affected their degree of cooperativeness although they also knew that in exceptional cases an extension of assignment time was sometimes granted.

At the end of the conference the new manager announced that he would supply details about the promotion policy and related matters in December. But when December arrived he said he had been too busy but that early in the new year he would definitely call a conference. However, it wasn't until April that he called another conference to discuss the promotion policy.

Soon after the (August) conference there were many earnest discussions, and there was unanimous agreement that research and design work was not subject to the kind of work measurement and methods techniques associated in most people's minds with the work of industrial engineers.

The idea that project engineers were going to be brought in was especially rankling, for many designers, particularly among those who worked closely with scientists, planners, and production on their projects, thought that they were already performing their duties, and what's more, relished their position. Furthermore, only a few weeks before the conference was called, a memorandum was sent from the chief engineer to the designers stating that designers were to act as "project engineers"—follow the project through from conception through testing and delivery.

THE INDUSTRIAL ENGINEER

When a group of IE's were hired in early October, they were doubtless bewildered to be met coldly and resentfully by almost everyone except the new manager and a few politically astute and alert types. To make room for these new engineers, desks, equipment, and files were moved out into the design-and-drafting areas from another room. There was just a little less room in some of the aisles, and design and drafting people subsequently resented the industrial engineers even more.

The industrial engineers began making inquiries about the work soon after arriving. It was obvious that they had direct access to the new manager, so overt uncooperativeness was not practiced. On the other hand, it was immediately clear that the industrial engineers were hardly at all versed in the kind of work that was being done—especially with regard to the technical aspects, not to mention the system by which the work got done. As a result, it was quite easy to confuse the IE's.

THE MEMO SYSTEM

One of the industrial engineers decided that the system of transmitting requests for desired alterations between design and production (by verbal instruction) was far from the way it was "supposed to be done." So one day the designers were called in to a conference with the chief engineer who informed them that alterations were now to be transmitted via written memo, and they were advised to keep a copy of such memos. Not only alterations, but also requests for revised estimates on production scheduling on one's design were to be transmitted via memo. Since no one was monitoring or enforcing the directive, this system broke down almost immediately. Also, Production refused to transmit memos to Design and Drafting for each revision and to commit themselves to anything but a conditional completion date.

TASK SHEETS

About November, after the industrial engineers had been in the Engineering Services Division for some time, the Engineering Design and Drafting Branch was instructed to fill in what were known as "task sheets." Designers and draftsmen were to keep a record of each part designed, giving a short description of the part (like "gear housing") and the number of hours spent on designing the part. This was extremely distasteful to everyone who had to fill in these sheets. The designers felt that the future use of the task sheets was obvious, and that their usefulness was far from evident in view of the fact that no two parts were ever built alike.

The task sheets were filled in, but were accompanied by long and bitter complaints ("I'm not going to get any work done now with all this paperwork," was the most frequent complaint). As soon as it was discovered that not all the sheets were being collected, and that their interpretation was indeed difficult or impossible, they were stopped abruptly. Nevertheless, from time to time the chief engineer would have the designers and draftsmen fill them in for he was requested to ask them to do so. But most designers and draftsmen plunked the sheets into the waste basket or "lost" them, and nothing happened.

OUTSIDE CONTRACTORS

During this period the chief engineer and his supervisors were continually asking for more men, particularly technicians, to help with the workload which was steadily increasing. Instead of hiring technicians, contract draftsmen were brought in beginning about December. Furthermore, the Design and Drafting and Production branches were urged to send work out on contract. The head industrial engineer, who had been with the division for some years was put in charge of contracting; and some of the new industrial engineers were made liaison men between engineering services, the outside contractors, and the research division. There was the same resentment and antagonism to the idea on the part of the Design and Drafting Branch, and also the Production Branch because, as it was generally expressed, this way of doing things would be more expensive (the government was supposed to be trying to save money).

The way the contracting was to work created another source of contention with the designers. The contracts were to be negotiated by the_industrial engineers, but the designers had to go along with the IE's and the contract designer to the research division's building and explain what was wanted by the scientists. Since the industrial engineers admittedly were not specialists in the research and design requirements, plans from the contractors were sent by the IE's to the regular design people who had to review the plans. This being the case, the question arose as to what would happen if the design failed to perform as proposed. If the design succeeded, the contractor would get the credit; if it failed, the designers would be blamed.

The designers also envisioned that if the design failed the industrial engineers could very easily turn around and ask why the plans had not been looked at more closely, calculations made, or mistakes caught, to which the designers could not reply "it was not my job." Also it was not going to be easy to point at the contract manufacturer unless there were obvious defects. Consequently much time had to be taken from in-house design so that the section supervisor and the designer could go over every detail very carefully.

PROJECT ENGINEERS ARRIVE

Since the new manager came, seven industrial engineers had come into the division, but by April 1969 three of them had left. This was a never-ending source of gleeful conversation among almost all personnel in the division. But in May. other changes took place that appeared to show promise of more long-range and lasting impact. This time a small group of three project engineers were brought in with a rank equal to the supervisors' of the design sections (the IE's were one rank below). They were knowledgeable about research work which their former companies were then doing, and this aroused keen interest among several scientists. The head of the Electronics Branch, who was widely respected for his technical knowledge as well as for his administrative ability, was made head of the project engineering group. Also, Design Section A's supervisor, considered the best engineer in the division, was transferred to the project engineering group.

The designers were puzzled as to what to do next. They could hardly ridicule the new group as a whole, since two of their most respected men were now part of the new group. Some decided to cooperate; others held out, reluctant to supply any information about the research division's work which was not specifically asked for. Little quarrels began to take place among designers. Hints and questioning tones about "betrayal" were aimed at cooperating designers.

The new members in the project engineering group were quickly learning their way round the organization, considerably aided by the two able oldtimers who were transferred to that group. It was interesting to note that as the new project engineers began to get accustomed to the place, the industrial engineers started showing vague expressions of dissatisfaction.

Discussion Questions

1. In the operations of the Design and Drafting Branch, lateral relationships were complex and varied. Carefully describe these lateral relationships. How would the complexity of the lateral relationships in the Design and Drafting Branch affect the developing of formal job descriptions of those working in this branch?

2. Much has been written about managing research and development operations. Because of the type of work involved, and the type of personnel attracted to it, research and development activities are expected to respond to certain managerial styles more than others. What type of style do you think would be most effective in the managing of research-and-development type activities? Why?

3. How would you assess the channels of communication, both formal and informal, in the Engineering Services Division?

4. Discuss the status of the designers before any of the changes were made. Do aspects of "professionalization" enter in here? If so, are they positive or negative? Discuss.

5. Trace the initial activity in the Engineering Services Division on the arrival of the new manager in July 1968. Was this reaction typical? In what way? Could management have done anything to alter the situation for the better? If so, what?

6. What effect did the changes proposed at the August 1968 conference have on the status of the designers?

7. Analyze the designers' reactions to the suggestions made at the August conference. What do you think their actions were "saying" to management?

8. What happened to the Industrial Engineers who arrived in October 1968? Why do you think this occurred?

9. What was the institution of the "memo system" implying about the work of the designers? Why do you think Production also was reluctant to cooperate as asked?

10. The designers indicated that the future use of the "task sheets" was obvious. What were the task sheets? Why do you think they were instituted? What was the obvious use feared by the designers? Do you think this fear was realistic? Why, or why not?

11. Why were the designers "gleeful" that three of the seven industrial engineers who had been hired in October of 1968, had left by April 1969? Again, what were they really saying?

12. Obviously management felt that the project engineers were the ideal solution to the problems encountered in the Engineering Services Division. What do you think? Why?

13. Why do you think professional people, or those who consider themselves as belonging to a profession, react so negatively to quantitative controls imposed on their work? Discuss fully. Is there any place for such demands in an organization such as this? Why, or why not?

14. The last sentence in the case should come as no surprise. Why? What is really going on here?

28

management problems
in india

My name is Cornelius, which may not strike you as an Indian name. My home is in Ahmedabad, where I have always lived. I work in Ahmedabad for an engineering company that makes water-drilling equipment. I have not been happy there, although my family wants me to continue.

My job in the firm is that of a production scheduler. I coordinate all the different departments of the firm, i.e., foundry, machine shop, assembly, testing laboratory, and inspection, to ensure the smooth running of the various departments with each other. However, it is not absolutely essential for me to visit all the departments and see the actual work in progress. I communicate with the various departments by writing "chits,"[1] giving full instructions, and then sending them by messenger to each department.

For example, when there is a shortage of some material in the machine room, it is brought to my attention. I write a chit to the storekeeper advising him of the shortage and requesting him to furnish the necessary goods to the machine room. Thus I am not "involved" in the actual transfer of goods but act as a link between the various departments. I have to plan all my work at least five days ahead because all departments have to be made aware of the production schedule well in advance. I have a tremendous amount of responsibility, for the final output is based on my decision. If my plans are not in line with the target set for production, or if I make a few bad decisions or calculations, production suffers.

[1]A chit is a small piece of paper on which instructions are given.

Unfortunately, full authority has not been given to me to handle the whole operation myself. When everything is running smoothly I have little to do; but when problems crop up I have to run to the manager or to the managing director for assistance.

Given my job as production scheduler, I am considered a supervisor. Thus I have no power over the machine-shop supervisor, or the storekeeper who is also a supervisor and on the same level as myself. This is rather sad, since I can only request the other supervisors to do such and such a thing and it is left entirely up to them to do as they please. I would not mind this setup if what they did could not affect me. But when anything goes wrong anywhere in the department I am the one who is held responsible whether it is my fault or not, since I am the production scheduler. This is what I resent the most.

I guess that to some extent it is my fault also. I do not go out of my way to see whether the machine room is functioning properly, whether the storeroom has adequate materials in stock, or whether the testing man has any complaints. I rely too much on my chits, and because everything appears to be okay on paper I assume that everything is also okay in the departments. My job is to coordinate and communicate via chits. And if my house is in order, I take it for granted that all is well around me.

The testing man thinks that I am too aloof; but I think that he is very unfair in his estimate of me. I would be the last person to show off my knowledge or superiority to my colleagues. I am known to have come from a rich family (probably because of the way I am dressed when I come to the factory) and I have no problems of transportation because I have a car which I drive to and from work. During the lunch hour my colleagues eat in the canteen, whereas I go downtown for my lunch. I never work overtime, and always have my weekends off.

The chief conflict between the other supervisors and me is that I have better qualifications. I have a B.S. degree, and they only have diplomas in mechanical engineering. I never try to show my superiority because of my better qualifications, but they feel inferior. What seems to irritate them most is that I happen to be a relative of the managing director (his wife's cousin, to be exact). The managing director hardly ever visits the factory. But whenever he comes I always have to accompany him and show him round the premises. I know this isn't good.

Glenn, the storekeeper, is a man in his early fifties and has five or six storeroom boys under him. He has risen from the ranks. He does not have much education (he was a high school dropout) but over the years he has learned a lot and has kept good control over his store. He is very attached to the company, probably because he is a widower, and works from seven in the morning until five in the evening. The storeroom is a second home to him. He never issues a new part or tool unless he is absolutely sure that the old one is useless and needs replacement. His policy is, "Do your work, and do it well, and I am your friend." He is a rule-bound man and a stickler for procedures. He resents a young man like me telling him things and giving him instructions, even by chits.

THE GRINDING WHEEL INCIDENT

Let me tell you about the most upsetting problem in which I was ever involved. It had to do with the machine-room operations. There were two supervisors in the machine room. One was Martin, the day-shift supervisor, who worked from 8:00 A.M. to 5:00 P.M., and the other was Robert, the night-shift supervisor, who worked from 5:00 P.M. til 2:00 A.M.

On one Thursday evening Robert had sent me a note saying that the grinding wheels had worn out and that it would be advisable to change them before the day shift on the next day (Friday). Since the note arrived late in the evening (5:00 P.M.) I could do nothing about it that day. However, the first thing I did the next morning was to send a chit to Mr. Glenn, the storekeeper, to replace the old grinder.

He promptly sent me a note (as he usually did) saying that the grinding wheels were not in stock. Knowing that no work could be done without the wheels I personally drove down to our suppliers during the lunch break, got the wheels, and had them sent to the storekeeper.

I thought for sure that Martin, the daytime supervisor, would install them that afternoon. But as I was to learn later, this was not the case. When Robert arrived at 5:00 P.M. that Friday afternoon, he noticed that the old grinding wheels had not been replaced. This upset him. After all, he had sent me a note twenty-four hours before about the situation. Anyway, he immediately removed the old grinding wheels and placed them on a conveyor belt that would take them to the waste-disposal area. After that he sent a chit to Mr. Glenn ordering new grinding wheels. It was about 5:10 P.M. at that time. The storekeeper refused to comply with the request saying that the storeroom boys had gone home for the day and that he also was doing the same. He locked his store and promptly walked off.

When Robert heard about this, he saw red. He could not do a thing about the whole situation. He could not get new wheels, and he could not get the old ones back because by that time they were in the junk yard. And without grinding wheels no work could proceed. As a result, he laid off his workers in spite of a heavy backlog of orders. Having nothing to do, Robert then walked off the job. It was 5:20 P.M. at that time.

I was working in my office that Friday evening, but as I was leaving the office to go home I bumped into Robert. I was completely unaware of what had happened during the past half hour. I had known Robert before I joined the organization. He was a few years my senior when we were in high school. Although I did not get along very well with him, when I met him outside the office I invited him to see a movie. He promptly accepted the invitation (much to my disappointment). We went to the movie theater, but since we did not get tickets we couldn't get in. So I invited him over for dinner. After dinner I dropped him off at his place, and as soon as I returned home I made a telephone call to my cousin (the managing director's wife) over some domestic issue, then I went to sleep.

The next morning (Saturday) I went to the office as usual. At this time I was completely unaware of the things that happened the previous evening. I guess Robert did not tell me anything because I did not ask him. Besides, I was under the mistaken impression that Robert must have switched shifts with the daytime supervisor and was going home when I met him.

Before I arrived that morning, the union officials had met the managing director over a complaint by the workers that they had been laid off the previous evening owing to lack of planning and coordination among supervisors.

Consequently an inquiry was held by the managing director. Glenn, Robert, and I were asked to present ourselves at the meeting. First the storekeeper was asked why there was no stock. He said that it was not a question about the stock being there or not, but simply that the request had come too late. The storeroom boys had left, and he had no idea where the goods were kept. (This was a blatant lie.)

Then Robert was asked the reason for laying off the workers. He said that he came into the machine shop at 5 P.M. and found the old grinders still in place. He wanted to know the reason why the grinders had not been replaced during the day shift, since the previous evening he had sent a note to me requesting me to replace the grinders. So far as he was concerned, the grinders had worn out, and so he threw them away and asked for replacements. The fact that his request was refused was not his fault.

When I was asked to tell my side of the story, I explained that I got Robert's original chit on Thursday evening, and I obviously could not have done anything about it that day. I got the grinders the next day, and had them sent to the storekeeper. I said that I had done my job, and I could not force the storekeeper to do his job for I had no authority to do so. My job was to see that the grinders were available, and it was Glenn's job to send them to Robert.

Management then asked me why I did not inform the day-shift supervisor first thing on Friday about the problem with the grinders. I said that immediately after the lunch break I had sent him a note informing him that the grinders were available in the storeroom, and he could replace them. (Of course the daytime supervisor might have felt that the nighttime supervisor would replace them, since the day shift was almost over.) I pleaded that although it was my job to coordinate the various departments, I could not force my ideas on any supervisor. I could only tell them about the situation, and it was their business as to what they did.

Robert was then asked about his unusual practice of discarding the old grinders and *then* asking for new ones. He said that since he was sure the new ones were available, he threw away the old ones and felt that what he was doing was right.

Glenn, the storekeeper, said that it was a premeditated scheme between Robert and myself to show him in bad light. He suspected that we had wanted to see a movie together, and to make that possible we had set up this whole incident. Apparently on Friday evening, when I was talking about the movie with Robert—after he had laid off the workers—some workers nearby had overheard our conversation. When Glenn came out of the building, he saw Robert and me driving away in a car. It was at this time that one of the workers had told him of our plans to see a movie. Glenn had known that Robert and I were just barely on speaking terms, and he was wondering why we had gone to the movies together. When I was accused of this I said that we had made no prearranged plans to see the movie. Besides, we were unable to go anyway.

While this was being discussed, the managing director (my relative) suddenly realized that I had made a telephone call to his wife, proving that I had not gone to the movies, although it was not a strong alibi. Glenn became increasingly irritated when he heard this because he felt that the managing director was trying to protect me by making up a story about the telephone conversation.

All in all, it was a most disturbing situation. Everyone was peeved at everyone else. Glenn was mad at Robert and me. Robert was peeved at Glenn, the daytime supervisor (Martin), and me. I was upset with the managing director for not having given me the authority to have ordered Martin to install the new wheels before Robert arrived. The managing director was upset with all of us. Besides, he had the union breathing down his neck. And to top it off, the workers in Robert's section were none too happy. The relationship between all the principals did not improve rapidly after this.

In retrospect, I feel that the basic problem with this organization was the lack of communication between the various people in the various departments. The management was really to blame, because it did not prescribe the exact job description for each individual. I was simply made responsible for too many things without being given the commensurate authority. All I could do was "request," when I should have been able to order! Maybe I was not the most personable fellow in the world, but at least I knew my job—which is more than could be said for some of the other people in the organization.

Discussion Questions

1. Do you think status and personal factors play a greater role in this Indian factory than they would in a comparable North American factory? Why, or why not? Cite examples from the case to illustrate your answer.

2. Do you think there is greater emotionalism and less business rationalism in this organization than in a North American company? Discuss fully.

3. How would you analyze the grinding-wheel incident? Who was really at fault? What changes would you suggest in operations to ensure that something like this does not happen again?

4. Comment on the writer's view of himself and his job. Is he correct about his authority not being commensurate with his responsibility? Why, or why not? Do you think that he should change his way of operations in some way? If so, how?

5. Analyze the lateral relationships between the various principals in this case—the writer, Glenn, and Robert. Do you think these relationships differ greatly from those found in North American corporations? Discuss.

6. What does this case tell you about conditions in companies in India? If you were sent to work in a company in India, what surprises do you think you might face?

29

introducing
a new appliance model

You have recently taken over as Division Manager of the portable TV Division of the X Electronics Company. Several years earlier this Division was a leading contributor to company profits; now it is losing money and can't compete with other domestic companies or imports.

Below is a simplified version of the organization chart of your Division:

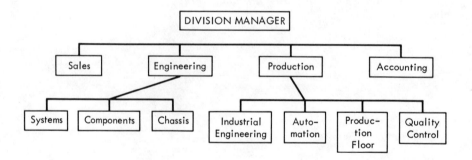

FIGURE 7
organization chart for TV division.

Your predecessor seemed to have good accounting records which enabled him to know on a biweekly basis when any group exceeded its budgeted expenses. You also have available daily production figures which enable you to spot problems in any area.

The work in your division encompasses the following

activities: Sales deals with customers (wholesale appliance dealers) and provides inputs to Engineering on what features (and what prices) are desirable from a marketing point of view; and Production, of course, manufactures the sets.

New models are introduced annually. This means that the Systems group develops the circuitry (the underlying electrical engineering of the new set). The Components group converts these specifications and design features into actual component and subsystem specifications (e.g., transistors, tubes, capacitors, et cetera). The Chassis group designs the cabinetry and frame. Industrial Engineering determines the specific production techniques and procedures that will be used. Automation designs and produces the equipment which makes the printed circuits and assembles components (with the goal of limited human intervention).

In reviewing past history, you note that the greatest problems seem to occur (and is not surprising) during the introduction of the new models. This past year was the worst. Sales noted a new trend toward bright, pastel-colored cabinetry. When the Chassis group was consulted on changing its design for the cabinet, it reported that the type of plastics that could be obtained in the desired intense colors could not be molded with the appropriate tolerances into the size and shape cabinet that had been agreed to. More rounding would be required, which would require the Components people to relocate one of their subsystems. They, in turn, said that this would have other impacts and they wanted additional time to calculate these and assess their costs.

At the same time Production was pushing for final plans, saying that every day's delay meant that their final tooling and training would be off by an extra two weeks. You found a memo from Engineering saying that over the years Production had stepped up their requirements for lead time (final plans to first models off the line) from two months to four months. Production's response had been that the promised simplifications in design had not materialized, and that budget cutting in various efficiency programs had reduced the number of production specialists they had to guide the work force in making a smooth transition from last year's to this year's model. At the end a number of fruitless meetings

177

were held in which Sales, Production, and Engineering endeavored to resolve their differences.

You found several other memos which indicated that the Systems group believed that the company's product was declining in quality; its reputation as the best in the industry was in jeopardy; and that good systems design was being sacrificed for what could be easily manufactured. They noted that the Automation group was harassing their design engineers, seeking to get a look at the early plans to see what they were like and to persuade the engineers to make modifications that would allow for greater use of automation, simpler printed circuitry, and more machine-controlled operations. This interfered with the design work and complicated it needlessly, noted the Systems manager.

Industrial Engineering said that there were a number of improved manufacturing techniques the company could employ if the Systems and Components people would call on them before introducing major new design features. Often minor changes in the design features would allow for very major manufacturing improvements. The Systems and Components group argued that Industrial Engineering sought to dominate these discussions, and that if they employed reasonable effort and ingenuity they could find ways of converting reasonable plans into manufacturing procedures.

It is obvious that as Division Manager, your predecessor had spent a great deal of time on the production floor during the early part of any new model year, and during the preceding weeks, trying to resolve bottlenecks and speed decisions. During this time there were apparently a number of problems like these:

Inspection shows a badly crimped wire likely to break during shipping and production. The Supervisor asks his boss to get the wire shifted, reinforced, or changed in some other way. Production head calls Engineering office to see if design can be changed. After locating the man who originally specified that subsystem in Components, answer goes back to Production that a change can't be made. By the time the answer gets back, a large number of sets are backed up waiting for change or release. Production head then requests that either quality standard (for breakage) be lowered, or that Division manager require Components to change their specs. Also he requests that Accounting modify its costing to take into account that Components' delay in responding slows Production. (It should be noted that one of the reasons for an almost automatic rejection of Production's requests for Component changes is that engineers have already been reassigned to new projects, and that redesign would hurt the Components' expense budget.)

Another observation you make is that the head of Automation is a very forceful personality who managed to influence the work of Systems by getting your predecessor to agree that certain aspects of the circuitry would be checked out with Automation before being finalized as part of the Division's efforts to reduce manufacturing costs. Whenever a problem arose the Automation group spoke with a clear, single voice. The head of Systems, on the other hand, was a rather mild-mannered, theoretically oriented engineer. He rarely spoke in the name of his group; but answered each charge or request in a very logical, systematic way. Over the past several years the company had lost a good many of its more ambitious circuit designers, and you wondered what was cause and what was effect.

Another problem revolved around the production methods and standards set by Industrial Engineering. When these seemed too tight to the production workers, the foremen often agreed with their men. Industrial Engineering would endeavor to get them accepted, noting that there was a learning curve and what seemed impossible at first, during the new model run, would seem easy after a few weeks. At times the workers would introduce "simplifications" in the job to meet the standard, and when these caused Quality problems at inspection time, it was not clear where the problem originated—from incorrect or ambiguous specifications by the Industrial Engineers, or the changes introduced by the workers or their foremen.

When Quality Control sought to have the problem investigated and the line stopped, the Sales group put pressure on Production to ignore this if dealer stocks had not yet been filled. At such times Production would argue that the company was dominated by a "sell now and don't worry about the product later" point of view, even though the company's market position had been attained through a combination of quality and technical pioneering. Sales reported that competition became keener each year, and that the end goal of the company was sales and not production.

Discussion Questions

1. Diagnose and describe the social system of this organization. Analyze the various lines of authority, communication, responsibility, work flow, and feedback which operate in this division. In other words, analyze what is happening in the TV Division.

2. Outline the steps that you, as the new manager, would take to make the operations of this division more effective. Be careful to distinguish between those elements that can be improved, and those that are likely to be unchangeable or difficult to change. Be certain to indicate where you are likely to meet resistance, and why.

3. Assume that you call in some outside experts to help you in analyzing and solving the problems in this division. Further assume that the following are some of the reports they give:

a. "The only problem is poor job descriptions. If every man knew his job, there would be no problems."

b. "The men at the head of each subdivision are simply not motivated to do the job."

c. "There is obviously a personality conflict between the head of the Sales and Production subdivisions."

d. "The problem is a typical one in large complex organizations, i.e., suboptimization."

Analyze each of these reports and indicate whether or not you think they might be valid, and why.

cynthia, the supervisor

For two years in the early 1960's, I was employed in one of the major banks in a city of approximately 100,-000 population in the Southwest. The bank employed about 80 people. I worked in the proof department, and was responsible for the local bank-clearing operations.

The proof department of a bank is so named because of its primary function of proving or confirming the accuracy of deposit slips received by tellers, checks entering the bank from other banks, and the cash transactions of tellers. All check and cash transfers are handled through the proof department. If errors are found, corrections are made and the parties involved notified. The proof department could well be called the check-sorting and routing department. The combined functions of routing, sorting, and proving are carried out mainly through the use of proof machines. Check-clearing is the transfer of checks between banks. Transit checks are checks received by our bank but drawn on banks in another city.

The proof department occupied an internal room with no outside windows or doors. Following is a floor plan of the room.

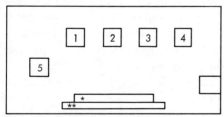

*   Working tables with adding machines.
**   Four-foot high divider.

FIGURE 8
floor plan of proof department.

181

The divider was about a foot wide, and served as a counter in transacting business. The divider also provided a "hallway" through the room for bank employees. This hallway connected the bookkeeping department with a hall that eventually led to an outside door. This line of travel was the main employee entrance to the bank and was constantly used. All machines and tables were so situated that every employee faced the line of traffic. This was done in order to economize on space in the room, but the positioning also gave the workers in the department the opportunity to glance up at the people passing through the room and thus did much to counter any feelings of isolation and confinement. Actually I feel that working in the proof room in the bank carried a certain prestige with it.

Cynthia was the proof department supervisor. Although she stated her age as twenty-eight, she could have passed for thirty-five or forty; she was single and looked it. I guess that my attitude toward her was always ambivalent—she was an amazing worker, but her personality often left something to be desired. She was not very gregarious, and seemed to find interacting with other people difficult.

Cynthia had worked her way up to the head of the department within seven years after she joined the bank. Her exceptional ability with the proof machines must have been a cause for this quick advancement. She was by far the fastest machine operator, and was most adept in all phases of our work. She could literally do the work of any two of the rest of us. When the workload in the department was heavy, she never failed to pitch in and work with us until the work was done. She was sometimes criticized for being so willing to pitch in and work with her subordinates, but this never seemed to bother her. As a matter of fact, Cynthia appeared to go out of her way seeking extra work. When a problem arose with our work, she would always be right there to help us solve it. Her skill and ability earned our respect, although we sometimes wished that she would spend more time explaining instead of doing.

From the above it may appear that Cynthia was always breathing down our necks. But this was not true at all. Actually she spent only about half of her time in our department. The remainder of the time she helped various departments in the bank to balance their books and find errors. If any department could not solve its difficulties, Cynthia would be called. She was the unofficial trouble-shooter for the bank. I can even recall that several times the president of the bank, usually trailed by some lower officer, came into the proof department to ask Cynthia a question. The question was often one which the lower officer should have known but did not.

Cynthia was so highly thought of with respect to her knowledge about the bank that she was once absent from our department for a week in order to explain the bank's operations to a seminar for bank examiners. I occasionally heard comments from other employees in the proof department that often Cynthia was not around when they needed her to solve a problem. I have never felt that way.

Cynthia was always a bundle of energy. If the work in our department was slow, she would bring in work from other departments. The supervisors of the other departments, although they welcomed the help, often were somewhat chagrined to see Cynthia bouncing in to "ask" for more work to do. The other supervisors felt that this implied criticism of their departments. This particularly worried these supervisors because they knew of Cynthia's close and frequent contacts with the upper management of the bank. It seemed that several times each day Cynthia could be found in the offices of the various vice-presidents, the personnel director, and the auditor, for private conferences. If anything was not operating as effectively as Cynthia thought it should be, she had easy access to those in charge.

Our proof department was the most efficient in town, and the speed with which we turned out our volume amazed other banks. Often on busy days we would have our work completed by the scheduled time of 4:00 P.M., and the other two banks wouldn't be ready. They would sometimes ask for a later time to clear; but since we were ready, Cynthia wouldn't grant the extension. The other banks would have to clear the checks they had ready. On the busiest days, our proof department employees finished and left by 5:00 P.M., whereas the employees of the other two banks worked until 8:00 or 9:00 P.M. If the other two banks made errors, as frequently was the case, Cynthia let them know about it.

Cynthia was a shrewd and difficult bargainer. The

other departments were always granting concessions to us, but we granted few concessions in return. For a few days, one of the other banks began picking up work from us early. If we had it ready we would give it to them; otherwise, if we were busy, we wouldn't stop to get it ready. After a few trips with no checks to show for it, the other banks lost interest.

Our proof machines were leased from a large office equipment manufacturer. All repairs were to be made by their service department which had two or three repairmen who served our local area. Almost every other day one of the five machines would be giving trouble. With a machine out of operation, our work piled up and our efficiency was impaired. Cynthia learned how to correct many of the minor problems while waiting for a repairman. Cynthia got along well with the repairmen if they arrived promptly and solved the trouble quickly. But woe to the repairman who had to return three times in two days to correct the same problem! Cynthia knew how and where to apply pressure, if pressure was needed to get things done. On one occasion, a call to the district service office got fast and efficient results. After the call, our local service was vastly improved.

Despite her many excellent qualities as a supervisor and worker, I still found Cynthia difficult to work for. She expected perfection in her subordinates, and did not hesitate to point out what she felt were lapses in performance. If she thought you were doing a good job, there was no problem and she would leave you alone. But if you were not doing a good job—watch out! Cynthia could "outcurse" any man in the bank! She felt no embarrassment in telling off other supervisors (at her own organizational level—or above) if she thought they were fouling up operations.

Cynthia's strong sense of business efficiency did not stop at the boundaries of our bank. Her relationship with the supervisors of the proof department of the other two banks in town was most unusual. Both these individuals were men and seemed, to me at least, to resent somewhat that a female—particularly a fairly young one—would have a position equal to theirs. At times I would be in the proof departments of the other banks when their supervisor called Cynthia. You could tell by the tone of their voices and expressions on their faces that they were extremely upset about a recent conversation with Cynthia. But they never seemed to confront her either over the phone or in person. No matter how incensed they might be over something Cynthia had said or done, when they started talking to her they became as meek as lambs.

Discussion Questions

1. How would you describe Cynthia's personality? How did her personality affect her performance? Give some other examples of how personality affects job performance.

2. Was Cynthia a good supervisor? Discuss fully. Would you have liked to work for her?

3. Discuss Cynthia's relationships with her subordinates, peers, superiors, and counterparts in the other banks. Did these relationships help or hinder the effective operation of (1) the bank, and (2) the proof department?

4. What do you think would happen to this bank if Cynthia left for some reason? Would this be beneficial to the bank? Why, or why not?

5. What effect did the fact that Cynthia was a woman have on her relationship with others, particularly the men? Do you think that Cynthia was "using" the fact that she was a woman in her relationships with others? Discuss.

31

the jungle
at foam brewing

The Foam Brewing Company is one of the nation's largest manufacturers of beer. It has its own malting plant in Rochester, and breweries in Queens, Binghamton, and Wilmington. The corporate headquarters are located at the site of the Queens plant.

The company is family owned and family operated. The organization chart appears below.

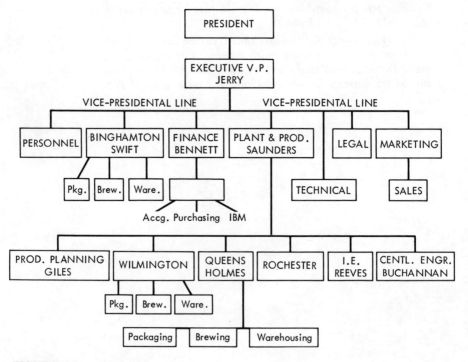

FIGURE 9
Foam Brewing organization chart.

186

The political situation among the top executives at Foam is filled with intrigue. Much time and effort are spent gathering data that will discredit the other executives on the same horizontal line.

The infighting at the top has resulted in the president being burdened with petty matters. Because of this, the president promoted his son Jerry to executive vice-president. Jerry had held the position of manager at the Binghamton plant. While he was Binghamton's manager, the rest of the vice-presidents agreed among themselves to let Binghamton do as it pleased. Thus Binghamton had its own accounting system, sales force, quality control standards, labor standards, and method of making the beer.

Now, with Jerry gone, Fred Swift was pulled out of retirement to take over at Binghampton. The seventy-year-old friend of the family was given the title of vice-president. However, he was not accorded the same freedom that Jerry had, and there have been innumerable squabbles between the staff at headquarters and the Binghamton-line people.

The general feeling within the company is that Swift's appointment is interim, and that the company is seeking to promote one of its division managers to the job. This has resulted in fierce competition and throatcutting among the middle managers.

The post of manager at the Queens plant is a newly created job. In the past the Brewhouse, Package Plant, and Warehouse managers used to report to the vice-president; now must report to a lesser man. This has created havoc at Queens because the managers feel they have lost status in relationship to the staffs that report directly to the vice-president.

On paper, this looks like an excellent move because now the many squabbles among the lines can be solved at a lower level. But this hasn't worked out, because Paul Holmes, the Queens plant manager, is not a capable administrator.

Holmes entered the organization as a brewing chemist in the technical department, and was pushed along by the family clique to brewhouse manager and ultimately to his new post. Technically he was expert only on the brewing phase, and deficient in packaging and warehousing. Thus he was looked down on by the latter two department heads as ignorant and biased. Holmes was an introverted man by nature and unable to cope with the more aggressive men who bypassed him and reported directly to Saunders. By permitting the managers to bypass him with their squabbles, he was able to eliminate the testy impersonal relationships he so abhorred.

Aaron Saunders, the Plant and Production vice-president, had a stated policy that Foam was not in the training business. If they needed a man to fill a job, they would steal him from a competitor by waving dollars at him. In order to keep the men, all division managers were on a dollar-incentive bonus system. Those who didn't produce were fired without notice.

Saunders' policy made fear and financial incentive the prime motivators. This led to severe competition among members of the production team and the staffs, and friction between the production staffs and financial staffs. The result was that most of the time and effort were spent in trying to impress Saunders and increase one's status in the organization instead of working for Foam.

When an open feud developed between Saunders and Bennett, the Financial vice-president, their animosity filtered down the line. Saunders used the Industrial Engineering Division to investigate shortages of raw materials and put the blame on Purchasing. He also used I.E. to audit accounting procedures. The Financial people retaliated by requiring the line people to fill out innumerable forms.

THE INDUSTRIAL ENGINEERING DIVISION

A brief description of the personalities of the members of the I.E. division follows:

HARRY REEVES—I.E. DIVISION MANAGER   Reeves took over the I.E. Division two years ago when Al Giles was promoted directly to Production Planning. Reeves immediately established himself as a hard-working and hard-driving executive. Between forty-five and fifty years of age, he was able to earn $30,000 a year including bonus. Reeves kept aloof from the men in the department and came to be regarded by the men as "stupid, selfish, and snobbish."

Directly reporting to Reeves were four senior IE's who headed the four responsibilities of the IE's. They earned between $10,000 and $13,000 a year.

JOE FRANCO—TIME STUDY AND STANDARDS SENIOR Joe
was the most respected of the Seniors, and was the informal leader of the work group. Joe, age 40, was admired
for his technical skills, general knowledge, forthright action. In addition, anyone who had ever worked under Joe
remarked that he was the best trainer they had ever had.
Joe had a reputation for being tyrannical, and didn't like
people to disagree with him.

BOB LATT—PROCESSING SENIOR At thirty, Bob was the
youngest Senior and least respected by the other Seniors.
Bob was what I would call a "daylighter"—his Foam job
was a supplemental means of income. His main income
came from royalties from inventions and full-length fea-
ture movies he made for commercial purposes. He earned
in excess of $50,000 a year. Bob was indifferent to Foam
and the status position of the Seniors. He did almost no
work at all himself, having delegated it all; but he was a
master at writing voluminous progress reports for Reeves.
Despite his apparent complacency Bob was very perceptive to the political situation around him and the limita-
tions of his authority.

JOHN NEWCOMB—WAREHOUSING SENIOR John was the
Senior man in the department. He was extremely status-
conscious and was ridiculed behind his back for wearing
white sox and a bow tie. He was not respected for his
technical ability.

CARL CURLEY—PACKAGING SENIOR Carl was known as the
"greaseball" because of his tendency to imitate Reeves in
a gross fashion. He thought he was the greatest person in
the world, but was not respected for his personality or his
technical ability.

Each department had a few Intermediates and Juniors
working for the Senior. They were directly responsible to
the Senior, and in most cases were recent university graduates.

LOU PRICE—INTERMEDIATE IN JOE'S DEPARTMENT Lou was
a hard worker, but wasn't too bright or perceptive. He
had an annoying personality, and was very status-
conscious. He was raised in a Pennsylvania coal town, and
attended Lehigh. He had an extreme dislike for the Ivy
League.

189

MAL COBB—JUNIOR IN JOE'S DEPARTMENT Mal was the playboy of Foam. His favorite expression, "Ho, hum," summed up his attitude.

ALBERT LANE—INTERMEDIATE IN CARL CURLEY'S DEPARTMENT Albert was the loudmouth of the department. He was studying for his Ph.D. in Operations Research at night. Despite his daily diatribe about Foam, his boss Reeves, and the big-money jobs awaiting him, he remained in the organization. He was favored by Reeves, and many believed that this was because he spied on the department for Reeves.

BILL FRANCIS—INTERMEDIATE IN JOHN NEWCOMB'S DEPARTMENT Bill looked like an executive, but had neither the desire nor the capabilities to be one. He was a passive individual.

RAY BRETT—INTERMEDIATE IN CARL CURLEY'S DEPARTMENT Ray was an easy-going fine man, aged thirty-five, and father of five. He was known as a "goof-off," but he was a competent worker when properly motivated.

RALPH RYAN—JUNIOR IN LATT'S DEPARTMENT Ralph was a very hard worker and took his job seriously. He worried quite a bit, and was very status-conscious. He was concerned with Reeves' and Latt's impression of him, and spent a good deal of his time worrying about symbols.

WARREN RITTER—MEMBER OF LATT'S DEPARTMENT Warren had worked for Foam for two summers, and was asked to stay on permanently and attend school at night. Reeves' personnel file described him as "able, strong, aggressive, a real asset to the company, with high leadership potential." Warren had a unique relationship with Reeves and Latt. He often stayed late to work overtime, and was able to have many informal conversations with Reeves. Latt hired Warren to work on his movie at night, and during the day gave him free rein to do as he pleased.

JOEL FOAM The boss's other son worked in Joe Franco's Department. Joel was considered the black sheep of the family. His father and his older brother Jerry had graduated from Princeton, but all Joel could do was flunk out of Rollins. Joel was not very bright or perceptive, but still exerted tremendous influence. At his father's request, Joel was spending a year in the I.E. department.

THE INDUSTRIAL ENGINEERING DEPARTMENT

The following is a brief description of the events that characterized Reeves's leadership of the I.E. department.

The I.E. department was started by Aaron Saunders soon after he took over as vice-president. The functions of Packaging and Warehousing were not typically I.E., and served to give the department a functional existence. The Standards and Time Study group was used as a political football.

The labor situation at Foam was unbelievable. The work force consisted of four times the number of men needed, and the union contract called for no layoffs and no compulsory retirement, a thirty-five hour week, 15 paid holidays including an employee's birthday. The Time Study group made exhaustive studies on all operations and prepared appropriation requests showing how many millions of dollars could be saved. Presumably Saunders presented these savings to Foam, and collected his bonus. But very few of these innovations and labor reductions were instituted because the union threatened to strike. Foam had suffered a crippling strike in 1956, in which the company lost 30% of its business and was unwilling to accept another at this time, thus the recommendations were filed.

Under Al Giles the morale of the department was very high. Giles maintained an open-door policy, and reviewed each project with the originating engineer at which time constructive criticism was presented. As Lou Price said, "When you made a mistake, Giles would let you know, help you correct it, and that would be that. He didn't hold a grudge—like this s.o.b. Reeves."

When Giles left the department the men felt bad. Reeves's initial actions didn't help matters. Reeves held a department meeting in which he stated his work rules and philosophy: "Only Seniors are to report to me. All reports that leave this department will be under my name. All contacts with upper management are to be made through me. Until the job is done, you are expected to work without overtime compensation. Gentlemen, the

191

I.E. department is the most important department in this firm. We must work as a team, and, above all, maintain good public relations."

Then, in rapid-fire order, Reeves discharged a couple of men and hired Bill Francis, Mal Cobb, Ralph Ryan, Ned Sutton, and Bob Latt. In doing so, Reeves changed the whole department. Ray was shifted from John to Carl. Ray was angry because he had quit his job at ConCan to get out of packaging, and now he was being put back into it. John was angry because Reeves had taken his experienced man away and given him a Junior. The hiring of Latt upset John and Carl because they thought that Bob was too young to hold a Senior's position. John expressed the belief that the role of the Senior was being downgraded.

Prior to the hiring of Sutton, once a week the Seniors used to meet for lunch at an expensive restaurant and discuss the department. John and Carl were especially annoyed with Bob because at lunch Bob didn't want to talk about business and preferred to talk about sex. When Sutton joined the company, Bob invited him up to the Thursday luncheons on the grounds that his age (forty-three) entitled him to it. John and Carl exploded, claiming that the role of the Senior had been reduced to nothing by Bob, and that henceforth they would not eat with Bob and his friends. After this outburst, Joe Franco dropped out of the lunch group.

A few weeks later, Reeves announced to the department that too much time was being wasted and that from then on there would be no more coffee breaks because the men had abused the privilege. He reasoned that he and Saunders didn't take breaks, and the men themselves shouldn't either.

The immediate reaction to this was that the men would get their own coffee at the cafeteria and drink it there, taking twice as much time. Finally Joe Franco went in to talk to Reeves, and Reeves agreed to have a morning coffee break, with the secretaries going to get the coffee, on the condition that it would be only a five-minute break and that each man was to stay at his own desk.

A month later Reeves sent Albert Lane and Carl Curley to California to look at other breweries. Curley told Lane to write the report, and that Curley would combine it with his and submit a joint effort. Lane, however, submitted his own report to Reeves. When Reeves received the same report from Curley, he called them into his office. When Curley still insisted that the report was his, Lane produced the handwritten copy and Curley was caught. The result was that Lane was transferred to John Newcomb's department.

About that same time, Lou Price went to Reeves to ask about his transfer to Binghamton as a resident I.E. Reeves replied he knew nothing about such an arrangement, and was not obligated to keep any promises Giles had made. Price left the office fuming, and made sure that everyone in the whole plant knew why.

A month later, when Ray Brett went in for his annual review, Reeves told him he wasn't going to get a raise because Ray had botched up the Wilmington project. Ray and everyone else knew that Carl Curley had botched it up and put the blame on Ray. Carl refused to go to Reeves and admit it, and Ray then dropped the matter.

During the summer, Reeves hired three college students as trainees. Bob Latt caused an uproar by the way he treated his man Warren Ritter. He gave Warren complete responsibility for several major projects, let him initiate any contacts he wished with whomever he pleased, and rewarded him with days off and expense account trips (including a five-day vacation to Miami Beach). Newcomb and Curley complained, and threatened Latt until they were blue, but Latt promised to reveal their cheating on expense accounts and days off if they didn't leave him alone. They replied, "Cheating on expense accounts and taking trips are compensations offered only to Seniors, and occasionally to Intermediates—but never to summer help."

When Reeves took off, he generally left a Senior in charge. However, when he left Curley in charge, Curley literally took over Reeves's office and assumed his job. Thereafter Reeves left nobody in charge, and consequently everyone else either took the day off or loafed.

In the fall, Saunders and Reeves instituted a suggestion system for the employees. Reeves announced to the department that they would evaluate the suggestions and modify them, but would not be eligible for any incentive because it was I.E.'s job to make suggestions. When foremen and other engineers started to get money for things previously suggested (and rejected) by I.E., morale hit an all-time low.

Harry Reeves's first annual review left the department in turmoil. According to the men, he refused to be specific and gave them double-talk when they asked for constructive criticism. Raises didn't necessarily go through on the basis of merit, but on Harry's personal opinion.

In February Reeves succeeded in getting larger quarters for I.E. But the men were very unhappy. In the old quarters, each department had its own office; but under the new layout only Seniors had private offices, and all the men were put in one massive open room where Reeves could look out at them.

Latt and Franco shared an office, as did Newcomb and Curley. Latt and Franco succeeded in getting their men located in the back where Reeves couldn't see them too well. Curley's men got the space in front, near Reeves.

At about this time, Joel Foam joined the department. He immediately became the focal point of the department. He was initially put in Franco's department, and both Franco and Latt constantly tried their best to make Reeves look like a fool in Joel's eyes. With Franco's prodding, Joel gave instructions for the coffee wagon to come up to the I.E. department in the morning. When Reeves found out it was Joel's idea, he gave in.

At the end of Joel's stay in Franco's department, Franco had to write a progress report to Joel's father. Franco told the truth, and the report made Joel look like an idiot. So Franco went over each item in the report with Joel, and told him how he could correct the flaws. Reeves told Franco to rewrite the report and mention only Joel's good points. Franco refused, so Reeves rewrote the report and signed it.

Thereafter, once a week Reeves took Joel to lunch. Joel reported to the men that while at lunch Reeves had asked him about the department, but that Joel told Reeves false things to make the men look good. A few weeks later, Joel was making regular trips to Saunders' office and his brother Jerry's office.

In a short span of time several significant things happened. Sam Ferraro, who was the mainstay and workhorse in Carl Curley's department, quit his job. Ned Sutton also quit. This left only Ray Brett in Curley's department. Reeves then shifted Lane back to Curley—with a promotion and a fat raise. The department tried to convince Brett and Lane to sabotage Curley once and for all. At the same time, Reeves placed an ad in the paper for an Intermediate without the department's knowledge. When the department Juniors found out they were angry because Price and Cobb thought they should be promoted. Both talked of quitting.

The next week Cobb quit, and Brett also started looking for another job. Two weeks later, Alice, a former I.E. secretary who had been fired by Reeves and was now working in Personnel, called to tell Brett that Reeves had filed to fire Brett on that Friday without any notice. The word spread through the department. Everyone was up in arms against Reeves and they convinced Brett to quit on Thursday, after the firing had been confirmed via the grapevine. Brett quit, and Reeves immediately told him to come back on Saturday to clean out his desk.

Last month, Reeves finally hired someone. To everyone's surprise, it was a Senior experienced in Packaging and Warehousing. Now Curley and Newcomb are afraid of losing their jobs.

Yesterday I spoke to Bob Latt, and he remarked that he also would quit his job as soon as he sold his latest movie.

Discussion Questions

1. There is considerable disagreement among organizational analysts about the effect family ownership has on a business. Some argue that it improves the operation because of the motivation to do well on the part of the family members. Others argue that nepotism and rivalries more than counterbalance the positive aspects of single family ownership. With regard to Foam Brewing, would you say that family ownership has been a positive or negative factor in the operations of the company? Discuss fully.

2. Examine the hierarchical structure at Foam, and indicate its strengths and weaknesses. Would you recommend any changes in the organizational structure? If so, what? Why?

3. What type of workers would a company like Foam attract? Why? Does it take a certain type of personality to withstand this kind of "jungle"? If so, what type?

4. Examine the motivational system in the organization as illustrated in this case. What kind of assumption is Saunders making about behavior in organizations? What effects has this had on the people and the organization? Would you change the system? If so, how?

5. What do you think of Mr. Saunders' policy toward training? What are the ethical issues involved in this policy?

6. Personality affects organizational behavior in various ways. How has the personality of each of the following men affected Foam Brewing: Paul Holmes, Aaron Saunders, Harry Reeves, Bob Latt, and Carl Curley.

7. What do you think of Reeves's initial statement of philosophy to his department? Why do you think he said this? What would be your reactions to such a statement?

8. How effective has the operation of the Industrial Engineering Department been under the leadership of Reeves? What indications are there that all is not well? To what extent can the difficulties with the Industrial Engineering Division be attributed to poor leadership on the part of Harry Reeves as opposed to other factors within the organization? What other factors could be causing these difficulties? All in all, would you say that Harry Reeves is an effective leader?

9. How would you assess the future of the Industrial Engineering Department under Harry Reeves's leadership? What do you think is going to happen?

10. What suggestions would you make to improve the situation at Foam Brewing? In the Industrial Engineering Department? What obstacles to change would you encounter at Foam? How would you attempt to overcome these?

a new division

At the Craig Company, a new division was formed that would be responsible for the corporate mining investments overseas. The objectives were to oversee mining investments in Africa; protect the company's interests in mining investments under construction in South America; and market iron ore throughout the world, especially in the Far East and in Europe. The long-term organizational goals were to maintain or augment dividend income from the African investments which were under increasing African political pressure to reduce dividends or reinvest in Africa; to handle all legal, financial, and managerial responsibilities involved in an iron-mine investment under construction in South America; to continue to market iron ore, and to develop new markets for the ore.

Senior management decided to locate the division headquarters at the main office, in a thirty-story building located in a major international capital. The corporate offices were on floors from the sixth through the sixteenth; but because of shortage of office space, a decision was made to locate the new division on the second floor. The existing offices of the president and vice-president were on the fourteenth floor. The offices of the Market Research section, composed of five people, were on the eleventh floor; part of the Commercial staff (four people) was on the sixth floor; the Engineers, (five people) and the Financial group (six individuals) were quickly moved to the second floor. The subgroups of the division were separated from each other physically by location on different floors of the building.

Since the new division was crucial to the operations of

the total organization, the president was to be the chief executive officer with his vice-president assisting him. Each of the new division's separate activities was to be headed by a managing executive who would supervise the people under him. Each of these executives was to report directly to the president or, in his absence, to the vice-president.

The president determined that the prime short-term goals of the new division were to concentrate on marketing iron ore and handle all details for the mine under construction. Management determined that a total work force of about 25 people would be adequate to accomplish all the work.

Before discussing the actual operation of the new division, it is necessary to make a few comments about the jobs of the president and vice-president of Craig Company. Because of the international operations of the company, both of these men spent less than half of their working time in their offices at corporate headquarters.

During the periods when the president and vice-president were in the office they were diligently preparing reports on their previous trips, catching up with correspondence which had accumulated during their absence, and making plans for the next trip. The periods spent in the office were short, two weeks at most, and therefore both men tried to accomplish as much work as possible by giving dictation not only to their own secretaries but also to the supervisors' secretaries. The supervisors resented having their secretaries become involved in this way because their own work fell behind. In order to complete the work, some overtime was required by the secretaries. The typing quality of the work for the executives was poor, because often the secretaries who were enlisted did not understand the dictation given by the officers and therefore did not type letters up to the quality standards expected by these men. The low quality work was returned to the secretaries for retyping. Letters and reports were retyped two or three times, and occasionally some work was redone four or five times.

The executives as well as the secretaries became irritated, and such irritation manifested itself among the girls by crying, grumbling, and refusing to work overtime, and by the executives in vocal outbursts. After a few months, one excellent secretary requested a transfer. Her reason for this request was that she had never before been a secretary to several people simultaneously, and she did not intend to begin now!

All groups should have moved to the new offices in September, but the offices on the second floor required major renovation before they could be occupied. From September until January no decision was taken on the floor-plan arrangement of the new offices. The president wanted to be consulted on all phases of the layout planning. But during those months he was away on business trips about 60% of the time, so there was little opportunity to discuss with him the details of the floor plan. The vice-president traveled with the president; consequently he could not be apprised of the layout planning being done by the engineers. No other group was requested to help with the layout, or make any decision on the plan, although all groups made suggestions.

At the time the division was formed, all employees were asked by the president whether a transfer would be acceptable. If anyone refused to leave his existing job, no penalty was assessed. Some who were invited did not accept because they believed—or so they said—that the new organization would not afford them the best opportunities. These people were not questioned further as to the reasons for their decision. Among those who joined the group were certain individuals who were dissatisfied with their present positions and had requested transfers. There were also others who had been suggested for transfer by their superiors because of unsatisfactory performance in their present positions. A few of these were accepted because they had the talents required, even though they had not done acceptable work in other positions. One or two of these had a long history with the company and previously had done fine work.

One transferee, a Market Research analyst, had been transferred from two other divisions prior to joining the Overseas Investment group. In the past he had done some superb analyses, but developed a reputation for being difficult to work with. He preferred to work alone, produced volumes of work some of which proved difficult to read because of unusual grammar and syntax. His approach to a job was imaginative and considered brilliant by his co-workers. He had never been promoted to a supervisory position when younger people around him were moved up. He claimed that the other employees had taken advantage of his special knowledge and used his work to advance their own interests. After a short period of time in each division, say three months, he became increasingly close-mouthed about the work he was doing and sent progress reports and final reports of his work not to his immediate supervisor for inspection, but to the senior man of the division.

Often the supervisor objected; but the analyst continued the practice. Resentful of his behavior, the supervisor refused salary increases or job promotions for this analyst. This had been his typical history prior to entering the new division. It was hoped that by transferring him, he would find satisfaction in the job and the company would benefit from his work. In the new division he was to report to the president. His job was analyzing and reporting on potential markets. Since the president was often absent, the analyst was subjected to little supervision and was soon working on pet projects unrelated to the work of the division.

From September to January he did almost no work that could have been useful to the president, and continually irritated the Marketing personnel who requested assistance from him and were refused; moreover, he constantly criticized the work of others. Eventually there was little conversation between the analyst and the others in the division. He claimed that his reason for not complying with their requests was that the work had not been initiated by the president who was, in fact, his boss.

OPERATIONS OF THE NEW DIVISION

Work efficiency in the new division was not high when the group was formed. Output was far less than expected. Most of the employees had not previously worked under the direction of executives; neither had the subgroups worked with their supervisors before. For some people, the type of work was different from what they had done previously. Also, employees were located on four separate floors.

Primarily the work involved calculation and accumulation of engineering, financial, and marketing data, and writing reports for the division executives and for the senior management. Advice of decisions approved or actions initiated by the division executives was relayed to the other workers vocally; however, when these men were out of the city, communication was in writing or by telephone. Frequently the executives made overseas telephone calls to keep the chief accountant, chief engineer, or other employees fully apprised of their activities.

Reports from subordinates were mailed to the executives when the latter were absent from the city. Reports from corporate headquarters were also mailed to the executives. Reports written by subordinates, however, were sent to the president and vice-president upon request and without approval of the traveling executives. Conflicts resulted when the travelers did not accept the conclusions in the reports, and in several instances subordinates were asked to retrieve the reports from the senior management so that they could be altered. The subordinates were greatly embarrassed on these occasions.

Communication between the offices in the building was accomplished almost entirely by telephone. A memorandum of instruction for normal day-to-day activity was time-wasting and unnecessary. Excessive time was consumed by the president, vice-president, and the division executives in traveling by elevator to the appropriate floors to give instructions, comment on work in process, provide trade-offs, or simply to observe what was going on. Often several trips each day were necessary for these purposes. In addition, employees were constantly traveling from floor to floor to pass on information, provide trade-offs, gossip, and report to the executives.

Telephones provided the most convenient way to communicate, but confusion and misunderstanding persisted. Errors in office correspondence and in reports to the president and vice-president became common. The uncovering of these errors resulted in anger or a feeling of frustration among the employees. Arguments between the subgroups which had cooperated to produce the reports became more frequent. Eventually the president and vice-president lost confidence in the work of the subordinates, and consequently also in the work of the division executives.

All groups attempted to take extra care to catch errors before the work left the office; yet, regardless of the amount of time devoted to eliminating errors, the instances of such errors did not diminish to any great extent. The total amount of work that would normally be expected ebbed as the writers and editors slowed in their output. Reports were produced late. A general lack of confidence in the work pervaded the entire office. The executives did not trust the subordinates, and the subordinates believed that the executives were exaggerating small errors. High-quality work, a goal of the executives and senior management, was not being produced.

Corporate management (the chairman of the board and some of the directors) also began to doubt the quality of work and pressured the president to insist on better performance from the new division. In turn, the result of this was that the president and vice-president became vocally abusive to division executives and employees, and to each other. Naturally enough, the problems continued.

As September passed into October, then November, there was a steady deterioration in work quantity and quality. Many employees spent considerable time just grousing together. The length of time spent traveling between floors to pass on information increased. One division executive began to arrive at work late and to leave early. His subordinates eased up on their work until he arrived, then slowed up again after he left. He began complaining to almost everyone who would listen. Some of his comments were: "The company has been unfair to me before on my job, and now they have shifted me to a new position where I won't be able to use my knowledge effectively." Or, "Now that I have this new job, which is a promotion, I expected to get a pay raise." Or, "The boss isn't here, and I don't know what I am supposed to do. He won't be back for a week."

In the four months that the division continued working on the four floors, morale among the employees disintegrated. A divisional esprit de corps had not developed. The few groups of three to five people who worked together on one floor, developed strong subgroup strengths. They worked together all day, and even had lunch together as often as possible. Each group was composed of people who did similar work. A kind of "professionalism" developed among the groups, especially in their supervised relationship with the division executives.

The president was absent from the office because he had to travel, but he was also "absent" from the employees because he believed that a certain distance should be kept between the supervisor and subordinates. He disliked administrative and personnel work, and avoided these activities as often as possible. It was his intention to have the vice-president handle these functions. The vice-president had a reputation for getting along with most people and tended to supervise using the "be good" approach, but he was not in the office enough to be effective. The president was autocratic in his dealings with subordinates and disdainful of the assistantship-type function of some groups, such as the corporate Personnel Department.

At the time the new division was formed, the vice-president was requested to fill out a job description of his work in the new division. The request emanated from the corporate Personnel Department. After completing the job description form, he asked the president to evaluate it. The president signed the form with the comment that the description of work was too elaborate, but that he would sign it anyway. Some months later, when the vice-president took an action with which the president disagreed, the latter questioned why the action had been taken without requesting permission. The reply was that the decision area for that work lay with the vice-president. The vice-president reminded the president of the job-description. The president then remarked that what was on the description form was for the Personnel Department, but that the form had nothing to do with what his job in the division was, so "forget the job description!"

The subgroups began to operate almost as separate companies with their own goals and objectives. After a few months, the differentiated groups increased the intergroup conflicts as trade-offs became difficult because of the physical barrier imposed by work done on separate floors. The flow of work, insufficient from the outset, decreased as conflicts increased and confusion between the groups arose. No cohesion between the subgroups existed, and inner subgroup cohesion developed to an excessive degree as the supervisors of each subgroup tended to represent only their subordinates' interests.

As this unhappy and unproductive situation wore on, top corporate management began to wonder whether the forming of the new division had been such a good idea in the first place. There was more and more talk that a complete reorganization of the new division was in the cards and, as rumor had it, "heads would roll." The president, vice-president, and division executives, feeling insecure about their jobs, were even more irritable and thus also inefficient.

Discussion Questions

1. Obviously, the Craig Company is a major corporation. How would you assess the company planning when it came to developing the new division? How would you have planned the development of the new division?

2. How effective were the modes of operation of the president and vice-president of Craig Company? It appears that their long absences from the offices were inevitable and necessary. Do you agree? Explain. What effects did the absence of these two senior officers have on the operations of the company? Of the new division?

3. The relationships between the top officers and their secretaries was not totally effective. How would you suggest that they should be changed? Who was at fault in this relationship?

4. The physical structure of an organization often profoundly affects its operation. What examples of this are evident in this case? What could be done to change the structure in order to improve the operations of this new division?

5. Analyze the staffing program developed for the new division. In what way was it effective? Ineffective? Would you make any suggestions for changes?

6. How would you assess the behavior of the apparently brilliant but troublesome Market Research analyst? How would you supervise his behavior? What is the best way to supervise a person of this type?

7. What kind of leader was the president? What was his style? Was he effective? How would you analyze his relationship with his workers? His vice-president?

8. Various operational problems developed in the running of the new division. Analyze each of these, and state the reasons, as you see them, for the difficulties, and what you would suggest to remedy the situation.

9. What do you think will happen in the future to this new division? Is the situation hopeless or not? Explain. Can anything be done? If so, what?